THE·CHILDREN'S
Visual Dictionary

Written by
Jane Bunting

Illustrated by
David Hopkins

DORLING KINDERSLEY
London • New York • Stuttgart

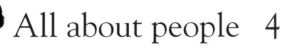

A Dorling Kindersley Book

Note to Parents

The Children's Visual Dictionary is packed with stunning picture definitions and a fascinating collection of words on diverse themes from *Mammals* to *Space*. The dictionary offers children a wide range of words, many of which are set in descriptive phrases, and includes less familiar words that name the special parts of objects illustrated.

Encourage children to learn how to use the book by looking up themes that appeal to their interests. The attractive photographs and illustrations will support children's understanding of new vocabulary. You can help your child by reading aloud together the words and captions that accompany the pictures. Help your children's understanding of words by talking about what they already know about a particular theme, and relating it to their own experience. Children will be able to draw on this broad range of vocabulary in their writing, both at home and at school.

The special word-finder index will help your child to learn how to look up words in alphabetical sequence – an important skill – and serves as a quick reference for checking spellings. Show your child how to follow page references for a word, such as "*body*", which may appear in different contexts. **The Children's Visual Dictionary** is a valuable language resource which will help to support children's development as readers and writers.

Olivia O'Sullivan and Ann Lazim
The Centre For Language in Primary Education, London

Project Editor   Monica Byles
Assistant Editor   Fiona Campbell
Art Editor   Peter Radcliffe
Managing Editor   Jane Yorke
Managing Art Editor   Gillian Allan
Production   Louise Barratt
Picture Research   Fiona Watson
Photography   Paul Bricknell, Steve Gorton

First published in Great Britain in 1995
by Dorling Kindersley Limited,
9 Henrietta Street,
London WC2E 8PS
Reprinted 1997

A CIP catalogue record for this book is available from the British Library.

ISBN 1-56458-881-5

Reproduced by Colourscan, Singapore
Printed and bound in Italy by Graphicom

Contents

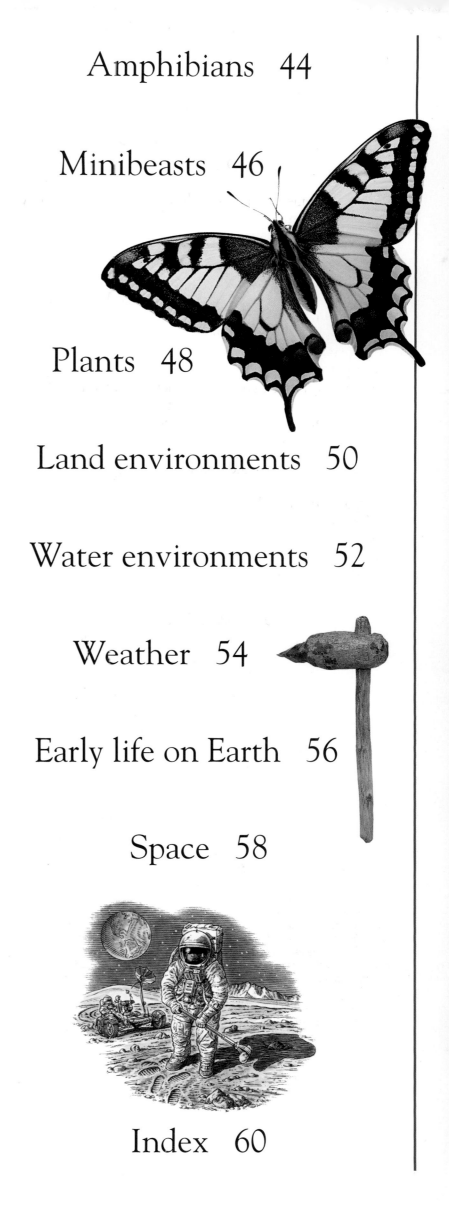

All about people

Human beings are special – we are the most highly developed mammal, and the only kind of animal to use words to talk to each other. Our brains control our bodies, allowing us to move quickly or slowly, think and remember, and express how we feel. As we grow up, our bodies gradually develop and change.

My family

father   mother   cousin   brother   aunt   me

My feelings

loving my puppy

twin sisters   smile

feeling shy

feeling happy

tears

feeling sad

frown

folded arms

feeling excited

feeling angry

Parts of the body

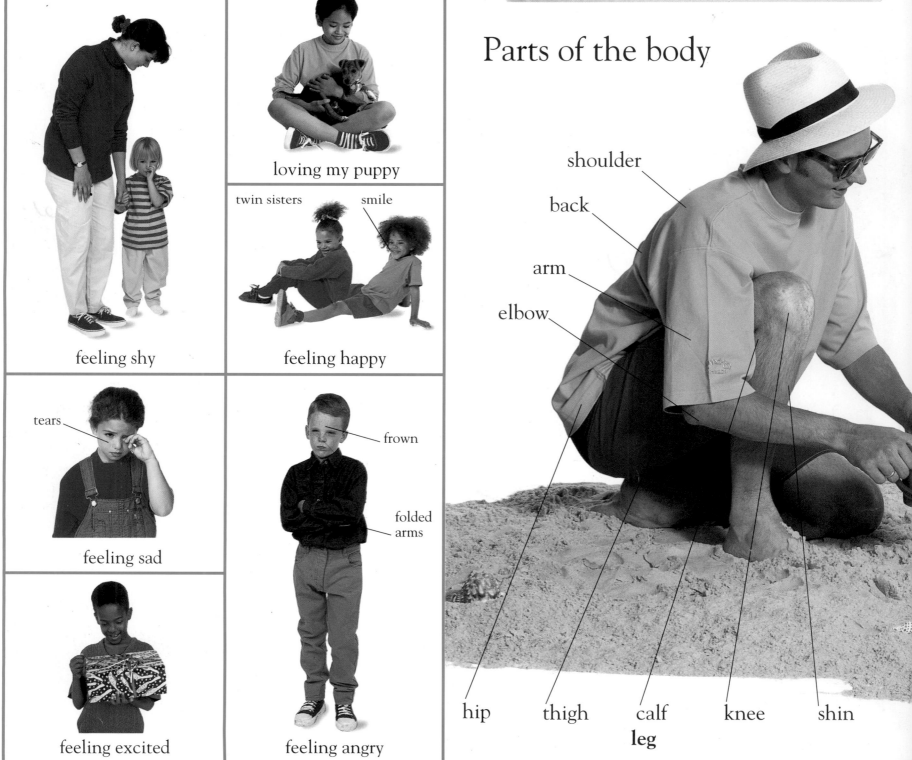

shoulder

back

arm

elbow

hip   thigh   calf   knee   shin

leg

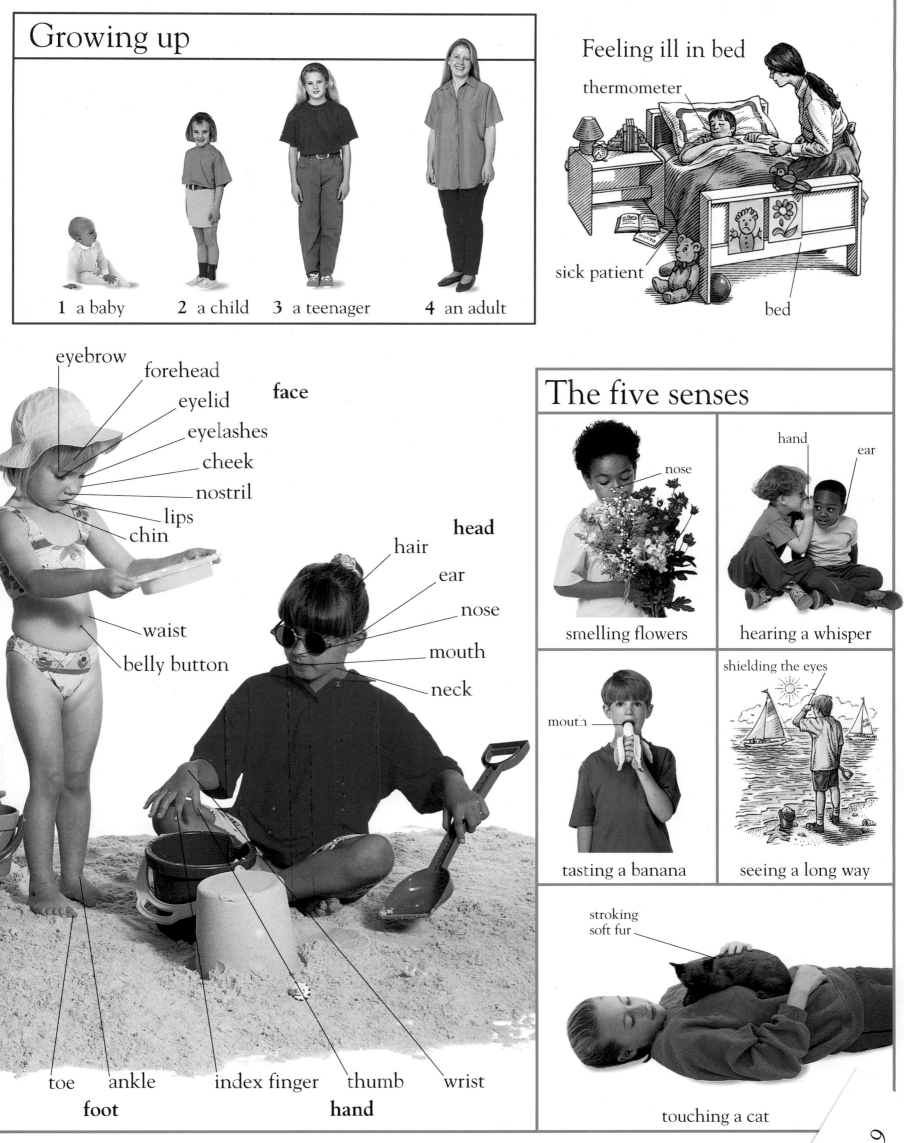

Growing up

1 a baby   2 a child   3 a teenager   4 an adult

Feeling ill in bed

thermometer

sick patient

bed

face

eyebrow
forehead
eyelid
eyelashes
cheek
nostril
lips
chin

waist
belly button

head

hair
ear
nose
mouth
neck

toe   ankle   index finger   thumb   wrist

foot   **hand**

The five senses

nose

smelling flowers

hand   ear

hearing a whisper

mouth

tasting a banana

shielding the eyes

seeing a long way

stroking soft fur

touching a cat

Going to school

In most schools around the world, teachers give lessons to classes of children. At school, children learn to read and write, and gain other skills and knowledge that they will need to live and work as adults. Schools also teach sports and recreational activities.

In the classroom

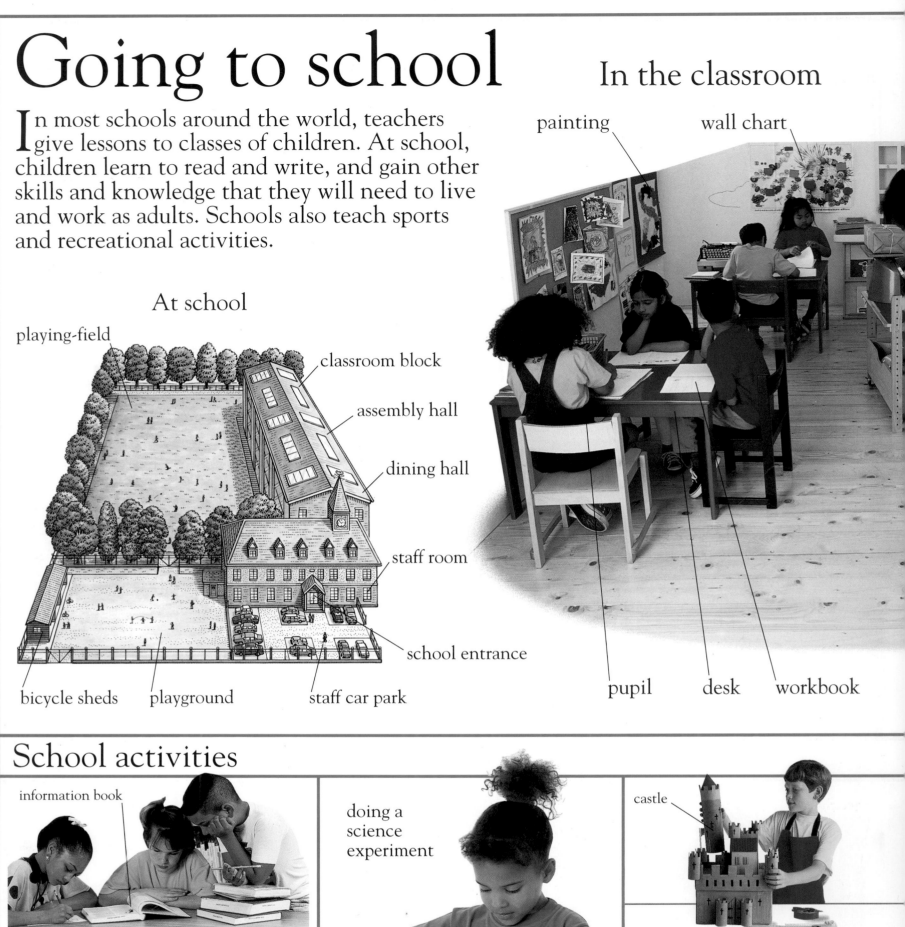

painting

wall chart

pupil

desk

workbook

At school

playing-field

classroom block

assembly hall

dining hall

staff room

school entrance

bicycle sheds

playground

staff car park

School activities

information book

looking at books in the reading corner

games teacher

sand pit

trying the long jump in a sports lesson

doing a science experiment

electrical circuit

castle

building a model

a geography lesson

world globe

resource area

project work on display

notice-board

resources trolley

teacher

Learning out of school

interviewee

project notebook

interviewers

doing research

pond

searching for minibeasts

ring-bound folder

working at home

display cabinet

fossilized dinosaur skeleton

visiting a museum collection

wheelchair

keyboard

monitor

compiling a database on the computer

compass

pencil

calculator

solving a maths problem

stage

curtains

scenery

audience

putting on a school play

overalls

painting

paint brush

paint pot

easel

painting a picture

7

People at work

Most people work so that they can pay for food, clothing, and a home for themselves and their family. There are many different kinds of jobs, some outdoors, and some indoors in places such as factories and offices. Workers such as doctors or firefighters help people in need.

At the vet's surgery

veterinary assistant

white coat

uniform

apron

pet dog

At the building site

hod of bricks

bricklayer

surveyor

foreman

cement mixer

scaffolding

carpenter

Different jobs that people do

bouquet of flowers

a florist in a flower shop

chef's hat

frying pan

a chef in her kitchen

computer

swivel chair

desk

an accountant in her office

water cannon

oxygen tank

firefighters putting out a fire

microscope

lab coat

a scientist in her laboratory

vet

pet owner

stethoscope

In the television studio

actress in costume

television monitor

actor

make-up designer

camera operator director sound recordist

The medical profession

dentist

doctor

mask patient

in the dentist's chair at the doctor's surgery

a hairdresser in his salon

scissors

comb

hair clips

potter's wheel

clay bin

a potter in his studio

overalls

tools

a plumber with her tool kit

screwdriver

foreman

car engine

assembly worker

conveyor belt

car factory workers on an assembly line

Going shopping

People shop for things that they want or need, such as food or clothing. At open-air markets, goods are sold from individual stalls. Specialized shops, such as bakers or hardware shops, sell only one type of merchandise. At supermarkets and department stores, shoppers can find all they need under one roof.

A busy fruit and vegetable market

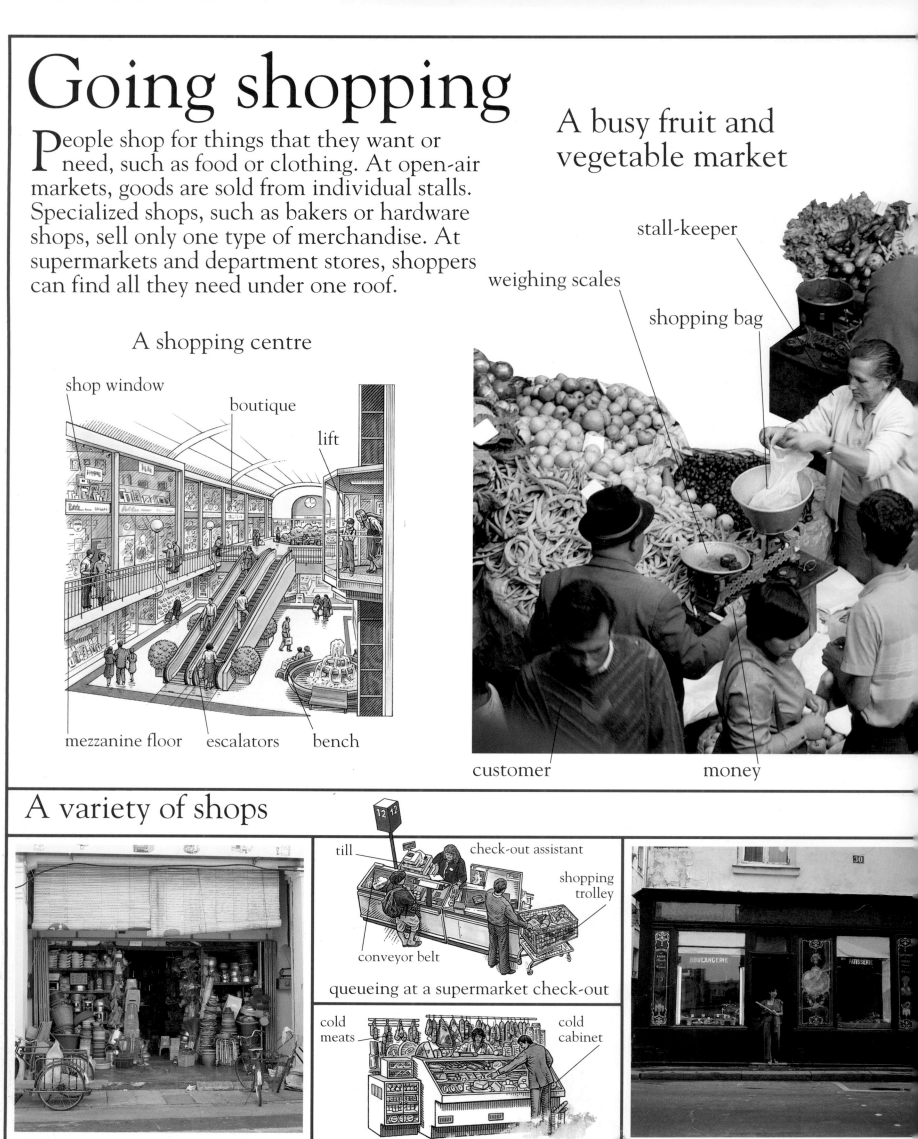

A shopping centre

- shop window
- boutique
- lift
- mezzanine floor
- escalators
- bench

stall-keeper
shopping bag
weighing scales
customer
money

A variety of shops

till
check-out assistant
shopping trolley
conveyor belt

queueing at a supermarket check-out

cold meats
cold cabinet

selecting food in a delicatessen

a hardware shop

leaving a baker's shop

shopper

storage basket

fresh produce

Customers in a toy department

shop assistant

merchandise

sales counter

shoppers

soft toy

display shelves

price ticket

shopping basket

crate

Shopping essentials

coin

a purse for change

straw basket

a shopping bag

bank notes   credit cards

wallet for notes and cards

note pad

pencil

a shopping list

living-room furniture

a display in a furniture showroom

newspaper

vendor

buying a paper at a newspaper kiosk

clothes rail

clothes hanger

clothes shop

computer terminal

holiday brochure

travel clerk

client

booking a holiday in a travel agency

Food and eating

All living things need food to stay alive. Food gives you energy, keeps your body warm, and helps you to grow. People enjoy eating many different kinds of food, both raw and cooked. It is important to eat plenty of fresh fruit and vegetables to stay healthy, and to have regular meals throughout the day.

A picnic

bottle of water

vacuum flask

bowl of crisps

jug

beaker of juice

plate of sandwiches

napkin

cloth

grilled sausages

An open-air café

parasol

order pad

diner

menu card

waiter

Food and drink

garnish
crispbread

a delicious snack

chopsticks

some steaming rice

drinking straw

fruit fool
teaspoon

saucer

a creamy dessert

a crunchy salad

orange squeezer

fresh orange juice

prawn
skewer

a tasty seafood kebab

sparkling apple juice

seeds

a juicy melon

barbecue grill tray

a sizzling fish

picnic hamper

fork   knife   plate   spoon

bunch
of grapes

strawberry

pineapple

salt and
pepper
shakers

**selection of
fresh fruit**

mug

bowl
of salad

Cooking food

a chef chopping
vegetables

white coat

chopping knife

chopping board

casserole
dish   apron

kitchen
scales

stirring some soup

weighing flour

dough

biscuit
cutter

mixing
bowl

saucepan   air
bubbles

cutting out biscuits

boiling some peas

baking tray

oven glove

baking a cake

balloon
whisk

apple
peeler

whipping some cream

peeling an apple

Tastes and flavours

sliced
pepper   gravy

black cherry

cream

a savoury meat stew

a slice of sweet cake

lemon peel

pith

salty peanuts

sour lemons

Hobbies and pastimes

People relax and spend their free time in many different ways, either on their own or with family and friends. Many people choose to go out for entertainment, maybe to watch a film in a cinema. Some people find fun in playing games or taking exercise outdoors, while others prefer to practise a hobby at home.

A puppet show

puppet theatre

audience

An adventure playground

ladder

wooden platform

rope bridge

landing mat

Outdoor activities

safety helmet

elbow pad

knee pad

roller-skate

roller-skating

hard hat

reins

saddle

stirrup

horse-riding

tent

rucksack

steps

diving board

swimming at an open-air pool

sleeping bag

torch

gas lamp

camping

backcloth

curtains

glove puppet

foreground scenery

Street theatre

stiltwalker

juggling rings

juggler

trick cyclist

stilts

unicycle

clown

Indoor activities

training shoes

disco-dancing

tiara

dressing up

reading a book

cinema seat

wide screen

watching a film

counter

dice shaker

boardgame

playing a game

kite

tail

string for steering

flying a kite

playing leapfrog

playing tag

tissue paper

scissors

making a collage

controls

playing a computer game

Music

People around the world play many different kinds of musical instruments, on their own or together in a band or orchestra. Depending on how they produce sounds, musical instruments are grouped into families – strings, woodwind, percussion, brass, keyboard, and electronic. Musicians either play written music, or improvise (make up the music) as they play.

Brass instruments

flared bell

piston valve

a French horn

music stand

trumpets in a brass band

slide

mouthpiece

a slide trombone

Percussion instruments

a percussion duo

tambourine

glockenspiel

beater

shake the maracas

cord

click the castanets

metal disc

handle

clash the cymbals

drum skin

beat the hand drums

wooden ridges

striker

scrape the guiro

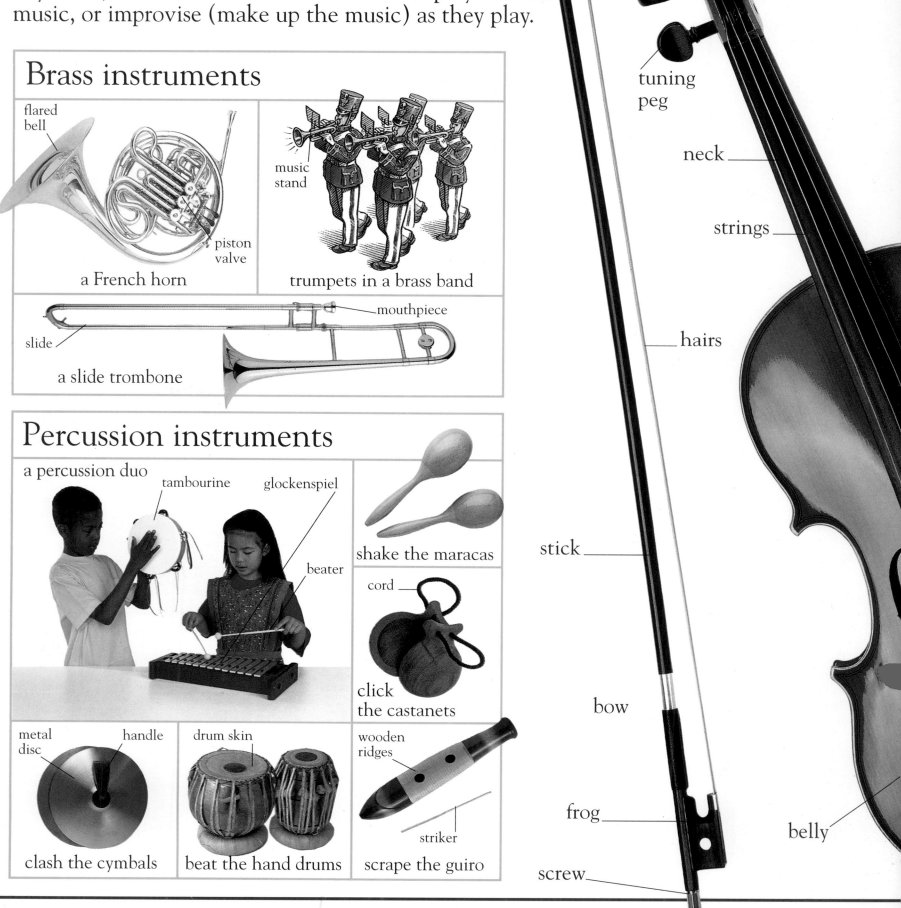

point   A violin

scroll

tuning peg

neck

strings

hairs

stick

bow

frog

belly

screw

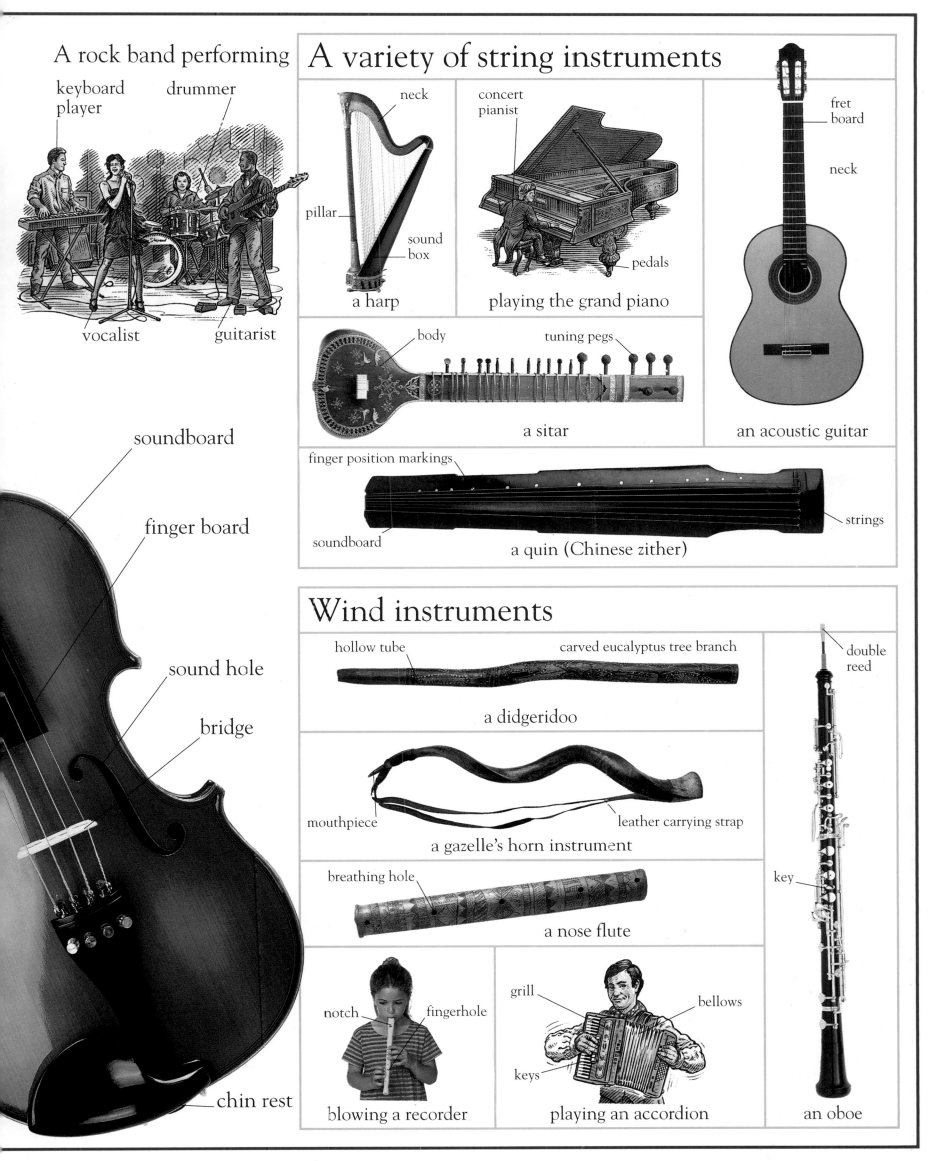

A rock band performing

- keyboard player
- drummer
- vocalist
- guitarist

soundboard

finger board

sound hole

bridge

chin rest

A variety of string instruments

- neck
- pillar
- sound box

a harp

- concert pianist
- pedals

playing the grand piano

- fret board
- neck

an acoustic guitar

- body
- tuning pegs

a sitar

- finger position markings
- soundboard
- strings

a quin (Chinese zither)

Wind instruments

- hollow tube
- carved eucalyptus tree branch

a didgeridoo

- mouthpiece
- leather carrying strap

a gazelle's horn instrument

- breathing hole

a nose flute

- notch
- fingerhole

blowing a recorder

- grill
- bellows
- keys

playing an accordion

- double reed
- key

an oboe

Sports

Sports are popular pastimes for many people. Players follow rules for each sport, and often use special equipment. In some sports, people try to beat other people's records. Many sports are team games, in which two sides compete.

A sports stadium

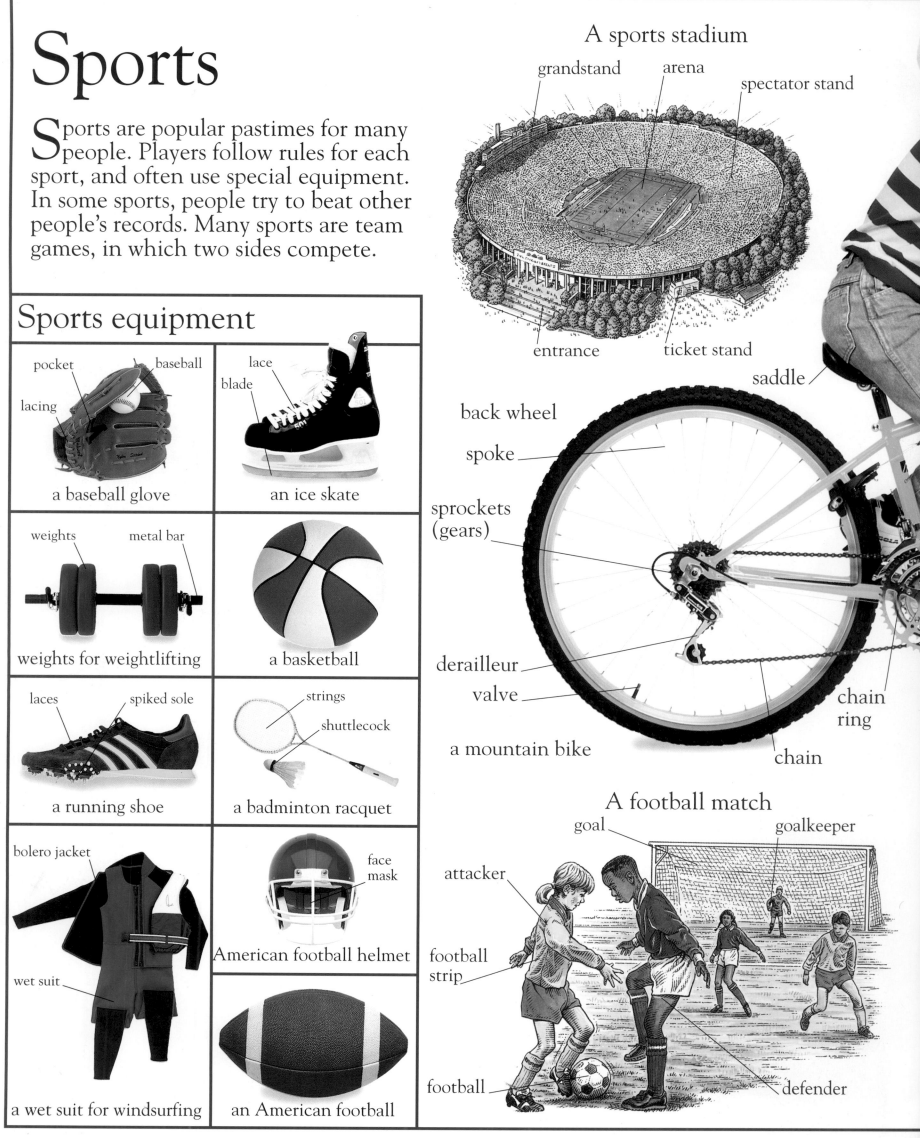

grandstand

arena

spectator stand

entrance

ticket stand

Sports equipment

a baseball glove
pocket
baseball
lacing

an ice skate
lace
blade

weights for weightlifting
weights
metal bar

a basketball

a running shoe
laces
spiked sole

a badminton racquet
strings
shuttlecock

a wet suit for windsurfing
bolero jacket
wet suit

American football helmet
face mask

an American football

a mountain bike
saddle
back wheel
spoke
sprockets (gears)
derailleur
valve
chain ring
chain

A football match
goal
goalkeeper
attacker
football strip
football
defender

A cyclist

- helmet
- chinstrap
- handlebars
- gear lever
- frame
- brake
- front wheel
- hub
- pedal
- tyre

Ball games

cricketer

cricket bat

batting in a cricket match

basket

shorts

basketball player

scoring in basketball

tennis racquet

forehand shot in tennis

tennis shoe

baseball bat

ready for the pitch in baseball

Some other sports

swimming

windsurfing board

sail

windsurfing

white suit

belt

throwing in judo

pole

ski

skiing

canoeing

paddle

canoe

Track and field events

judge

the high jump

sprinting

throwing the javelin

hurdling

Where people live

A stone castle

Everyone needs a place to call home, where they can feel safe, shelter from the weather, and store their possessions. Homes around the world are as different as the people and families that live in them. Usually, they are built from whatever materials can be found locally – mud, wood, brick, or stone.

Life in the city suburbs

high-rise apartment block

brick terraced house

avenue

detached house

front garden

pavement

Homes built on water

wheel house

chimney

cabin

a flat-bottomed houseboat barge

ladder

window

stilt support

wooden long-houses on stilts

tower

weather vane

bell tower

finial

steeply pitched roof

turret

skylight

arched window

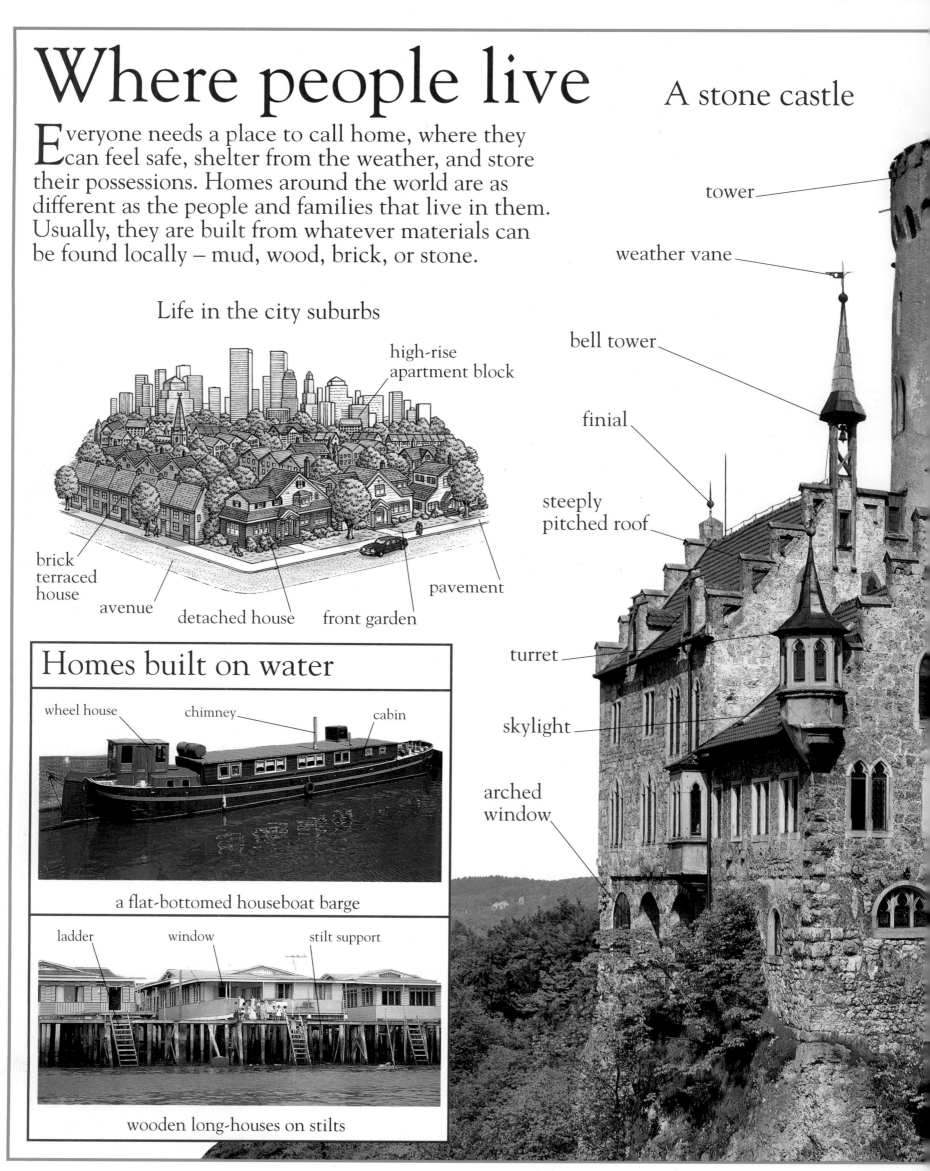

battlements

Homes in the country

flat roof

a mobile home in Australia

window door path

cave dwellings in Turkey

guy rope fabric roof

a Bedouin tent in the desert

stitched skin tent guy rope

a yurt in Mongolia

thatched roof mud wall

Ethiopian thatched huts

balcony sloping roof

a chalet in Switzerland

gate-house

Homes in the town

window eaves

television aerial tiled roof porch

a bungalow

a concrete tower block

a house with a courtyard

21

Towns and cities

Cities and towns are busy places, with streets of houses and other buildings, where many people live, shop, and work together. These large communities often provide public services for the inhabitants, such as the police, fire brigade, hospitals, and libraries.

A city scene

skyscraper

office block

apartment building

taxi

ice cream vendor

A city square

street lamp

parking zone

street signs

one-way road system   fountain

Places of worship

minaret

a mosque

bell tower

a cathedral

domed roof

a synagogue

statue   columns

a temple

City services

fire engine

a fire station

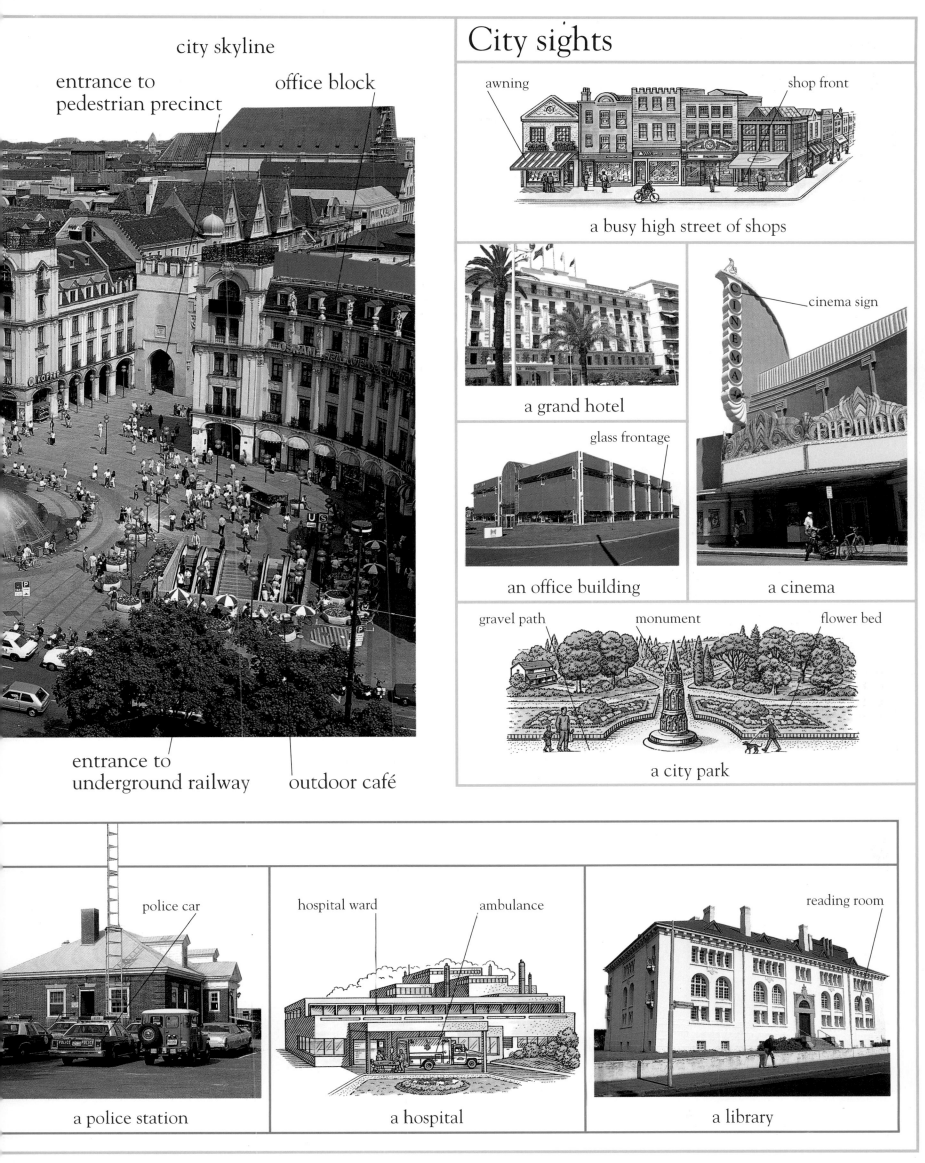

city skyline

entrance to pedestrian precinct

office block

City sights

awning

shop front

a busy high street of shops

a grand hotel

glass frontage

cinema sign

an office building

a cinema

gravel path

monument

flower bed

a city park

entrance to underground railway

outdoor café

police car

a police station

hospital ward

ambulance

a hospital

reading room

a library

On the farm

Much of the countryside around the world is used as farmland to grow crops and to rear animals. Farms produce food all year round, as well as materials such as wool and rubber. Although some farms are large, mechanized industries, many remain small and are run by families in traditional ways.

A dairy farm

a tractor ploughing · hay barn · grain silo · farm house

wheat-field · cattle grazing (eating grass) · farmyard · milking parlour (dairy)

Harvesting crops

tea bushes

picking tea leaves

combine harvester

harvesting wheat

rubber tree

tapping rubber

A tractor working the land

tractor driver

cab

exhaust pipe

engine

tyre

power harrow

hub

Farm animals

herdsman

calf

a herd of cattle lowing

pannier

a donkey braying

woolly coat

a llama snorting

gosling

a gaggle of geese honking

nanny goat   horns

beard

kid

two goats bleating

comb

wattle

a cockerel crowing

sheep dip   farm hand

sheep dog

a flock of sheep bleating

Planting rice in a paddy field

irrigation pit   rice terrace

farm worker   rice seedlings

furrowed earth   roller   furrow press

Farm produce

carrot

egg   cheese

radish   sweet potato

butter

root vegetables

dairy foods

grapefruit

lemon

orange

lime

citrus fruit

barley   rye   oats

cereals

25

Travelling by road

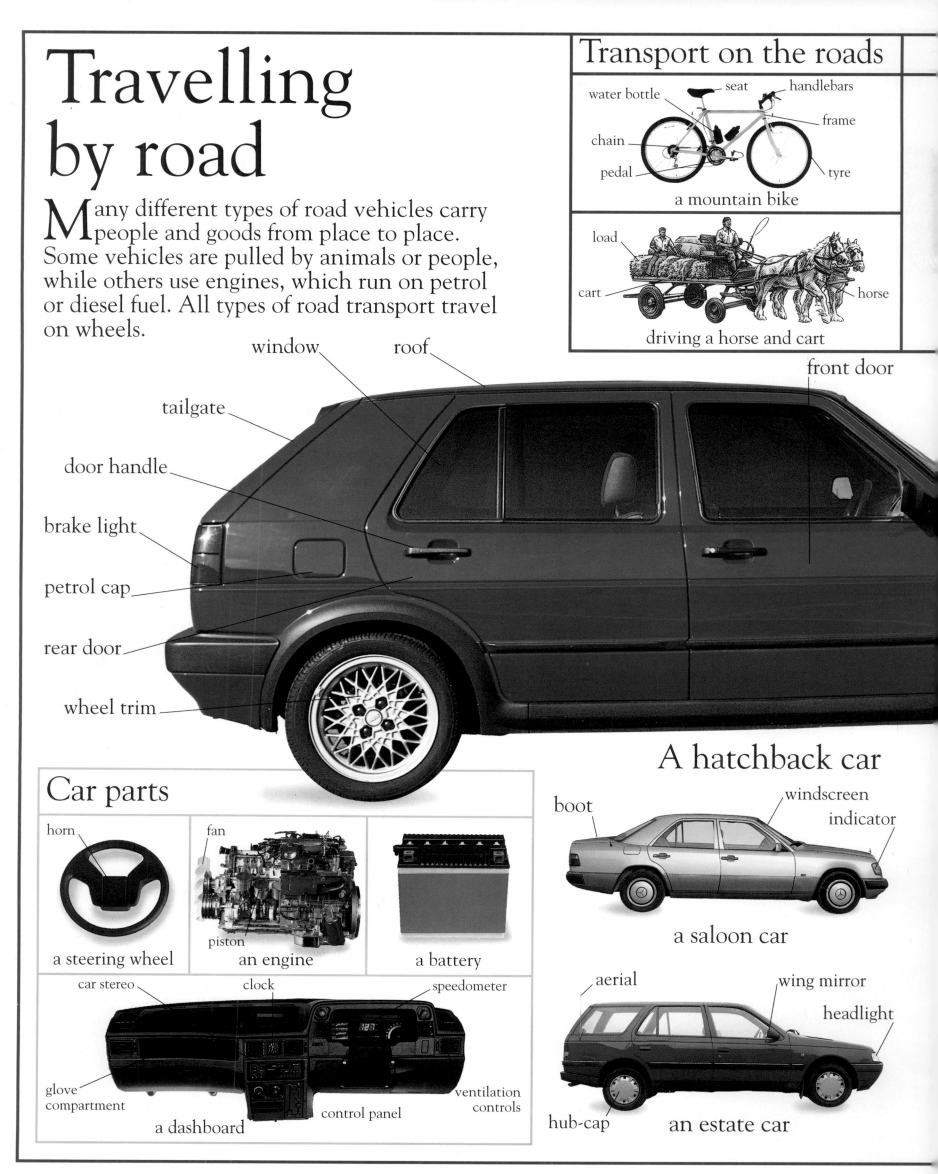

Many different types of road vehicles carry people and goods from place to place. Some vehicles are pulled by animals or people, while others use engines, which run on petrol or diesel fuel. All types of road transport travel on wheels.

Transport on the roads

water bottle
seat
handlebars
frame
chain
pedal
tyre

a mountain bike

load
cart
horse

driving a horse and cart

window

roof

front door

tailgate

door handle

brake light

petrol cap

rear door

wheel trim

Car parts

horn

fan

a steering wheel

piston

an engine

a battery

car stereo

clock

speedometer

glove compartment

control panel

ventilation controls

a dashboard

A hatchback car

boot

windscreen

indicator

a saloon car

aerial

wing mirror

headlight

hub-cap

an estate car

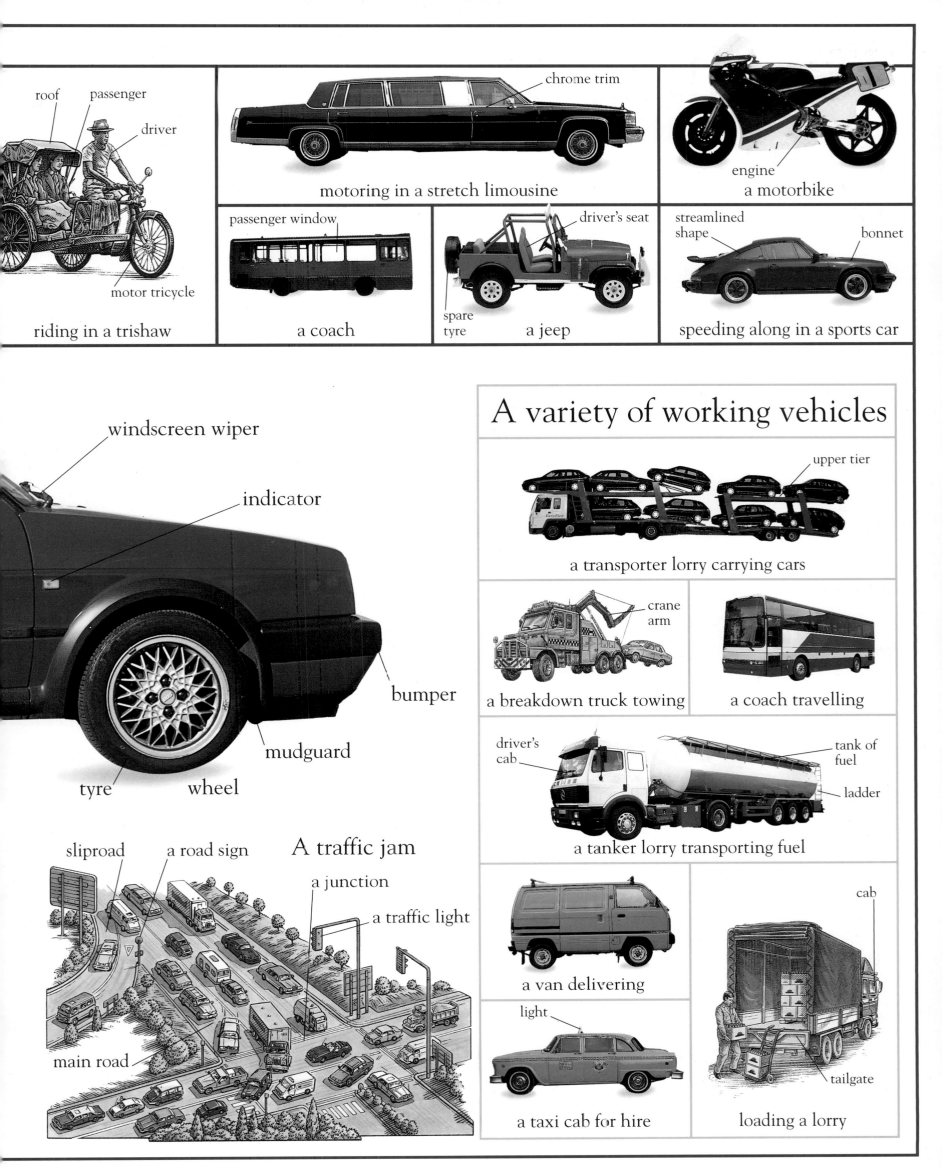

roof
passenger
driver
motor tricycle

riding in a trishaw

chrome trim

motoring in a stretch limousine

engine
a motorbike

passenger window

a coach

driver's seat

spare tyre
a jeep

streamlined shape
bonnet

speeding along in a sports car

windscreen wiper

indicator

bumper

mudguard

tyre   wheel

A variety of working vehicles

upper tier

a transporter lorry carrying cars

crane arm

a breakdown truck towing

a coach travelling

driver's cab

tank of fuel

ladder

a tanker lorry transporting fuel

a van delivering

cab

A traffic jam

sliproad   a road sign

a junction

a traffic light

main road

light

a taxi cab for hire

tailgate

loading a lorry

Travelling by rail

Large numbers of people use trains to travel quickly from place to place. Trains are also used to transport heavy loads. For many years, trains ran on steam, produced by coal burning in their engines. Nowadays, many trains run on diesel fuel or electric power, which runs either through electrified tracks or through overhead wires.

signal ticket office waiting-room
timetable
ticket inspector
railway track
platform
porter
luggage

At a railway station

carriage window

Inside an observation car

driver's cab horn
windscreen ladder insignia
headlight
fender

A variety of trains

an electric train speeding

windscreen wiper

a diesel train engine

headlight chimney coal tender

a steam locomotive chuffing

a bullet train hurtling

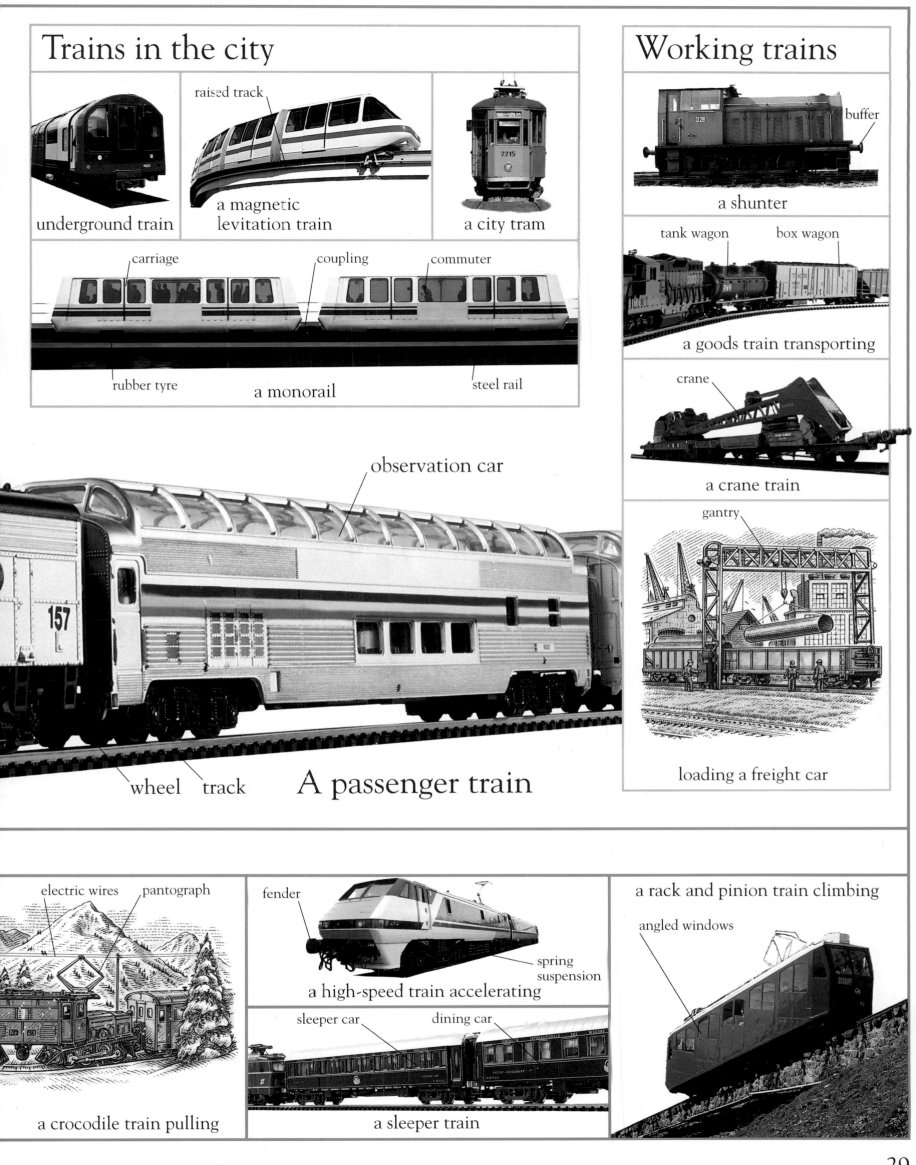

Trains in the city

underground train

raised track

a magnetic levitation train

2215

a city tram

carriage   coupling   commuter

rubber tyre   a monorail   steel rail

observation car

157

wheel   track   A passenger train

Working trains

D26   buffer

a shunter

tank wagon   box wagon

a goods train transporting

crane

a crane train

gantry

loading a freight car

electric wires   pantograph

a crocodile train pulling

fender

a high-speed train accelerating

spring suspension

sleeper car   dining car

a sleeper train

a rack and pinion train climbing

angled windows

Travelling by sea

All sorts of ships and boats travel on the sea. Some have sails and are driven by wind power, while others have engines and carry cargo and passengers over long distances. Boats unload their cargo in a port or harbour, a sheltered place on the coast where they can drop anchor safely.

Ship's equipment

a sextant

a steering wheel

an anchor

rope

a life-buoy

The harbour

lighthouse

harbour wall

lifeboat station

crane

warehouse

quay

slipway

Ocean liner

radar mast

lifeboat

bridge

porthole

bow

anchor

hull

PACIFIC PRINCESS

Ships and boats

gun turret

helicopter pad

a frigate patrolling

oar

outrigger

an Indonesian canoe floating

mainsail

spinnaker

a yacht heeling

container cargo

a container ship unloading

periscope

conning tower

a submarine diving

propeller

a hovercraft skimming

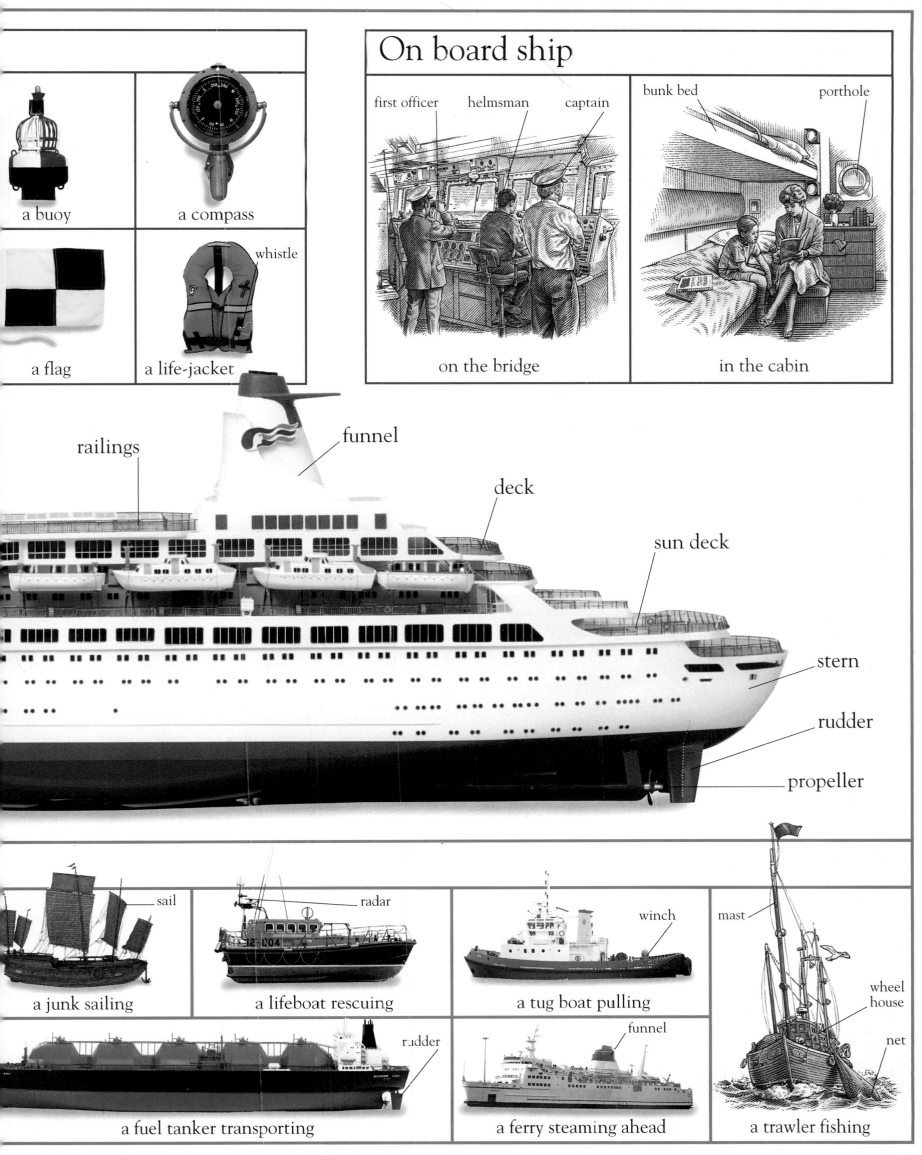

a buoy

a compass

a flag

whistle

a life-jacket

On board ship

first officer helmsman captain

bunk bed porthole

on the bridge

in the cabin

railings

funnel

deck

sun deck

stern

rudder

propeller

sail

a junk sailing

radar

a lifeboat rescuing

winch

a tug boat pulling

mast

wheel house

net

rudder

a fuel tanker transporting

funnel

a ferry steaming ahead

a trawler fishing

Travelling by air

The Wright brothers flew the first aeroplane in 1903. Since then, flying has made it easy for people to travel long distances fast. There are many types of aircraft that people now fly either for business or pleasure.

a stunt aeroplane

coloured smoke trail

An acrobatic air display team

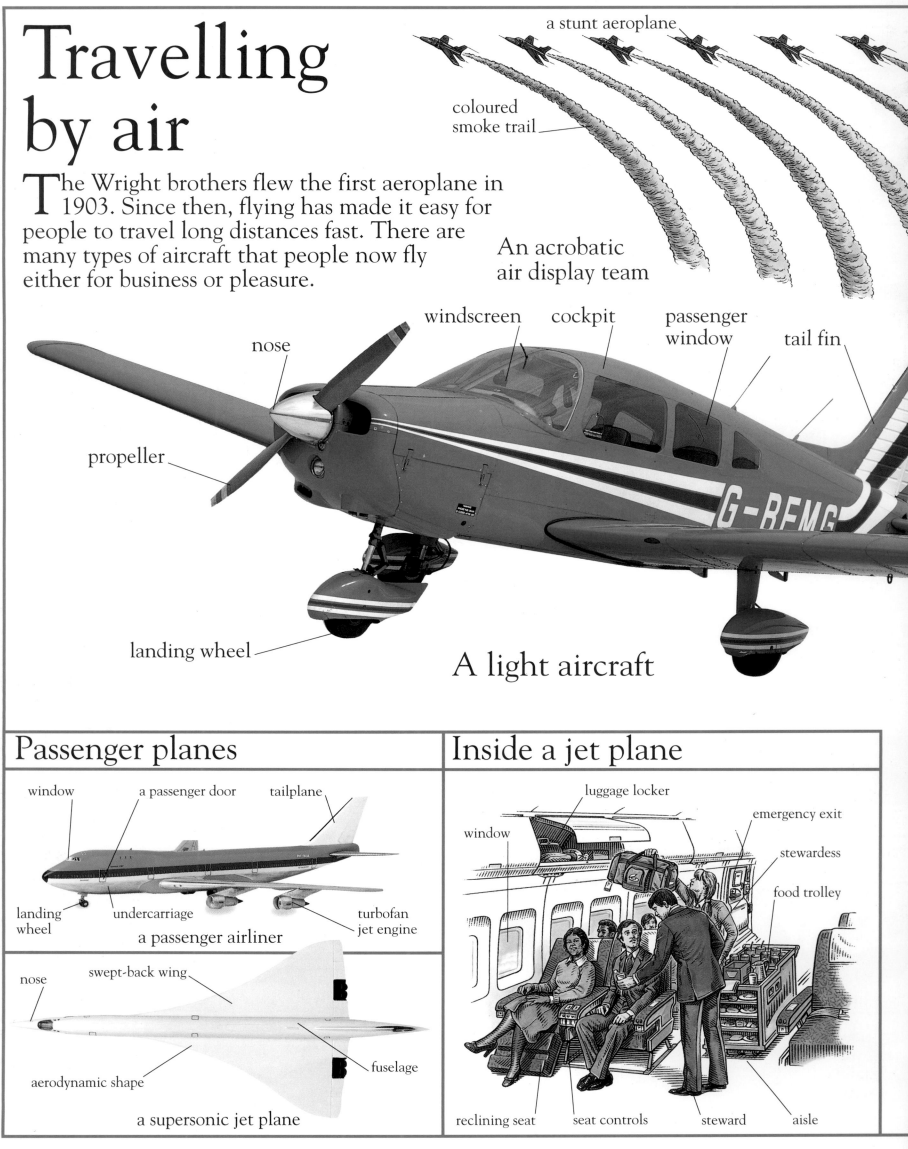

windscreen

cockpit

passenger window

tail fin

nose

propeller

G-BFMG

landing wheel

A light aircraft

Passenger planes

window

a passenger door

tailplane

landing wheel

undercarriage

turbofan jet engine

a passenger airliner

nose

swept-back wing

aerodynamic shape

fuselage

a supersonic jet plane

Inside a jet plane

luggage locker

emergency exit

window

stewardess

food trolley

reclining seat

seat controls

steward

aisle

Flying for fun

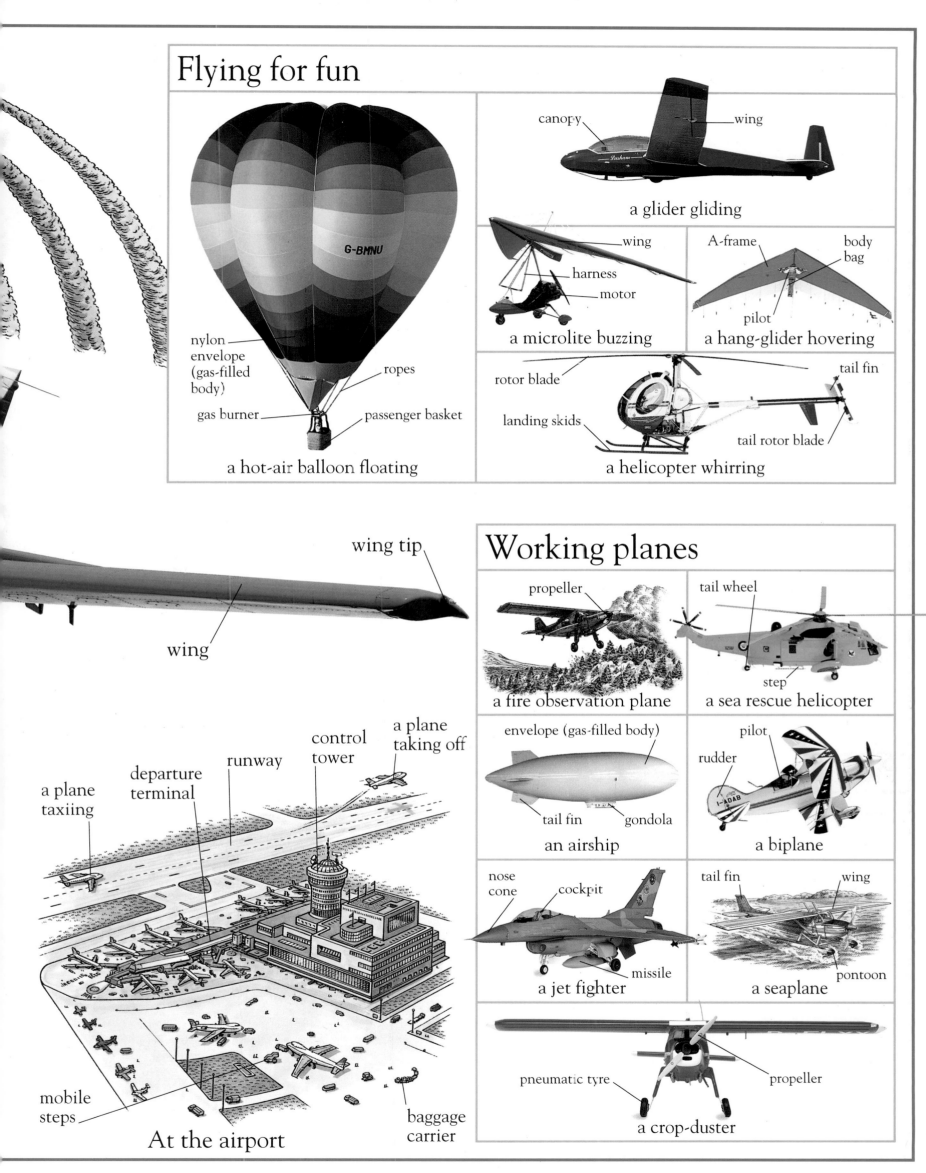

canopy — wing

a glider gliding

wing
harness
motor

a microlite buzzing

A-frame — body bag
pilot

a hang-glider hovering

nylon envelope (gas-filled body)

ropes

gas burner — passenger basket

a hot-air balloon floating

rotor blade — tail fin
landing skids
tail rotor blade

a helicopter whirring

Working planes

propeller

a fire observation plane

tail wheel
step

a sea rescue helicopter

envelope (gas-filled body)

tail fin — gondola

an airship

pilot
rudder

a biplane

nose cone — cockpit
missile

a jet fighter

tail fin — wing
pontoon

a seaplane

pneumatic tyre — propeller

a crop-duster

wing tip

wing

a plane taking off

control tower

runway

departure terminal

a plane taxiing

mobile steps

At the airport

baggage carrier

Mammals

Mammals are warm-blooded animals that give birth to live young. The parents look after their young and feed them on milk. Mammals are usually covered with hair or fur. They use lungs to breathe and are intelligent animals with large brains. Human beings are mammals.

A bat

large ear

finger

wing membrane

claw

ear

eye

nose

tongue

shoulder

arm

stomach

finger

toe

A macaque monkey

Mammal heads

trunk

an elephant

tusk

snout

fangs

a fox

whiskers

a sea lion

mane

forelock

a camel

muzzle

nostril

a horse

flipper

beak

A school of dolphins

A pride of lions

mane

lioness

lion

cub

furry coat

leg

tail

Mammal coverings

striped fur for camouflage

a tiger stalking

spotted coat

hoof

a fawn trotting

three toes

shaggy hair

a sloth hanging

sharp quills

a porcupine scurrying

tough, leathery hide

horn

a rhinoceros chewing

mother giraffe

dappled skin

calf

scutes (armour plates)

bristles

an armadillo hunting

a giraffe calf suckling

Mammal homes

dried grass

feathers

branches

a squirrel in its drey

baby moles

nest

tunnel

a mole in its underground burrow

Reptiles

Reptiles are scaly-skinned, cold-blooded animals, such as snakes. Some reptiles live in water and some live on land. Most reptiles live in warm parts of the world. They use the warmth of the sun to give them energy to move. Young reptiles hatch from eggs.

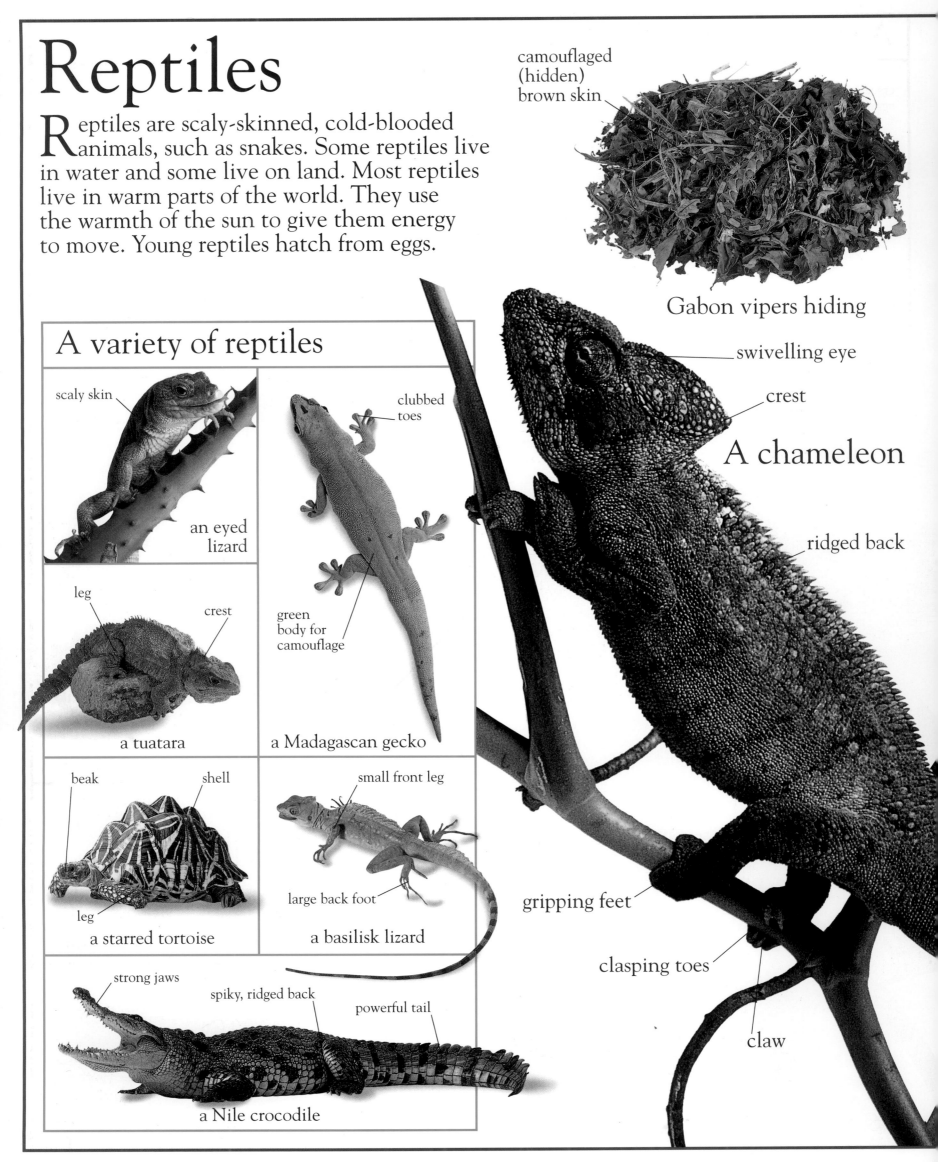

camouflaged (hidden) brown skin

Gabon vipers hiding

A variety of reptiles

scaly skin

an eyed lizard

clubbed toes

green body for camouflage

a Madagascan gecko

leg

crest

a tuatara

beak

shell

leg

a starred tortoise

small front leg

large back foot

a basilisk lizard

strong jaws

spiky, ridged back

powerful tail

a Nile crocodile

swivelling eye

crest

A chameleon

ridged back

gripping feet

clasping toes

claw

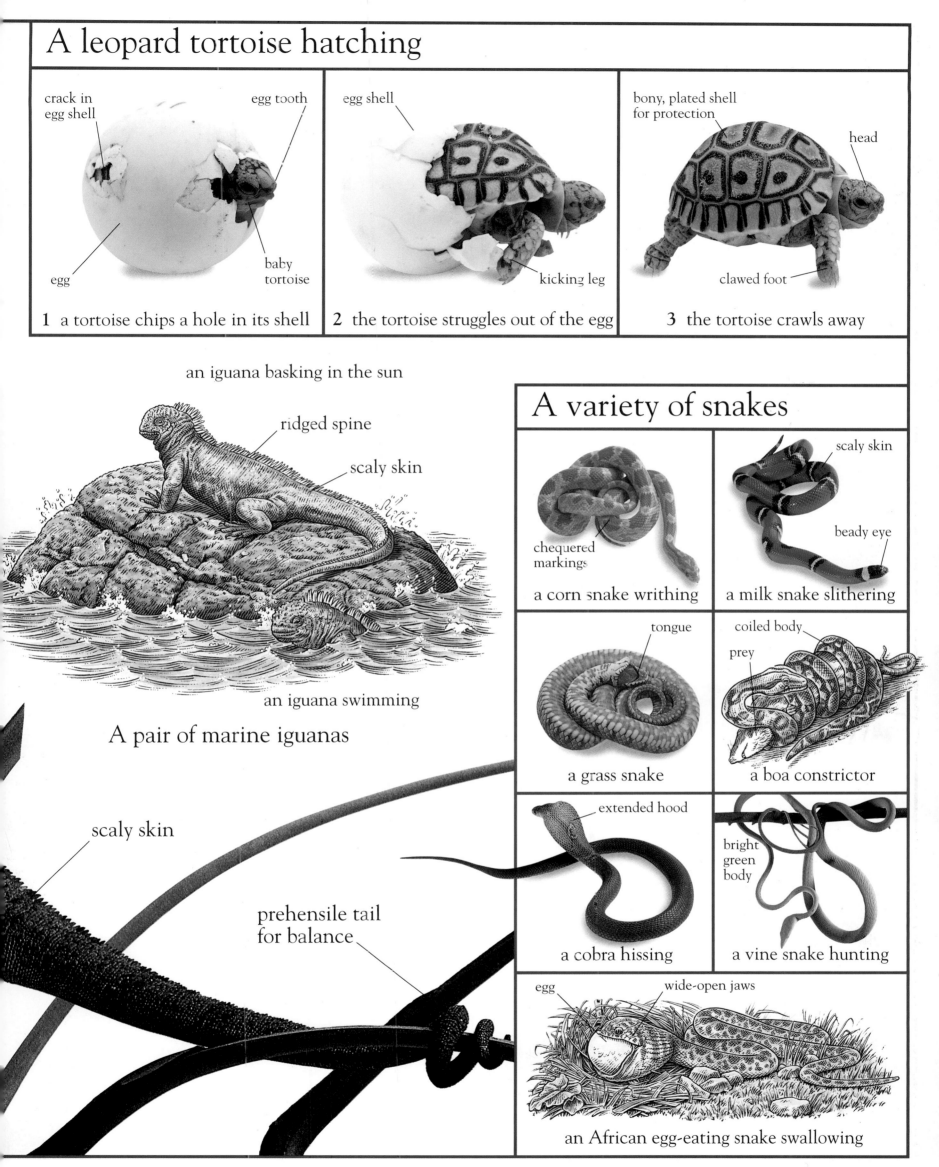

A leopard tortoise hatching

crack in
egg shell

egg tooth

baby
tortoise

egg

1 a tortoise chips a hole in its shell

egg shell

kicking leg

2 the tortoise struggles out of the egg

bony, plated shell
for protection

head

clawed foot

3 the tortoise crawls away

an iguana basking in the sun

ridged spine

scaly skin

an iguana swimming

A pair of marine iguanas

scaly skin

prehensile tail
for balance

A variety of snakes

chequered
markings

a corn snake writhing

scaly skin

beady eye

a milk snake slithering

tongue

a grass snake

coiled body

prey

a boa constrictor

extended hood

a cobra hissing

bright
green
body

a vine snake hunting

egg

wide-open jaws

an African egg-eating snake swallowing

Birds

Birds come in many shapes and sizes. All birds have wings, but not all of them can fly. Birds are the only animals that have feathers. They also have beaks and lay eggs.

A red-fronted parrot

nostril

head

eye

hooked beak

nape

breast

belly

leg

ankle

foot

toe

claw

Beaks

flat bill

a shelduck

hooked beak

an imperial eagle

short, thick beak

a goldfinch

curved beak

a toucan

long beak with a stretchy pouch

a pelican

curved bill

a flamingo

Growing up

feathers   hair

moss   grass

1 a nest with blue tit eggs

shell   egg-tooth

2 hatchlings

feather tufts

3 young nestlings

feathers

4 fledglings

Macaw feathers

shaft

barb

quill

a flight feather

soft down feathers

body feathers

wing

tail

A variety of birds

wing feather

talons

an owl swooping

sharp beak

a kiwi hunting

beak

claws

tail

lorikeets preening

comb

egg

a hen nesting

nectar-drinking beak

a hummingbird hovering

a Japanese grosbeak finch perching

long neck

knee

webbed foot

a flamingo wading

a skein of geese migrating

flipper

iceberg

waterproof feathers

A group of penguins

a blue pigeon flying

fantail

fanned tail

a peacock displaying

Sea creatures

Many different creatures live in the seas and oceans of the world. Most sea creatures breathe through gills, although some fish have lungs. Fish are the largest group of animals that live in the salty waters of the sea. Many other creatures live on the seabed, on rocks, or on the seashore.

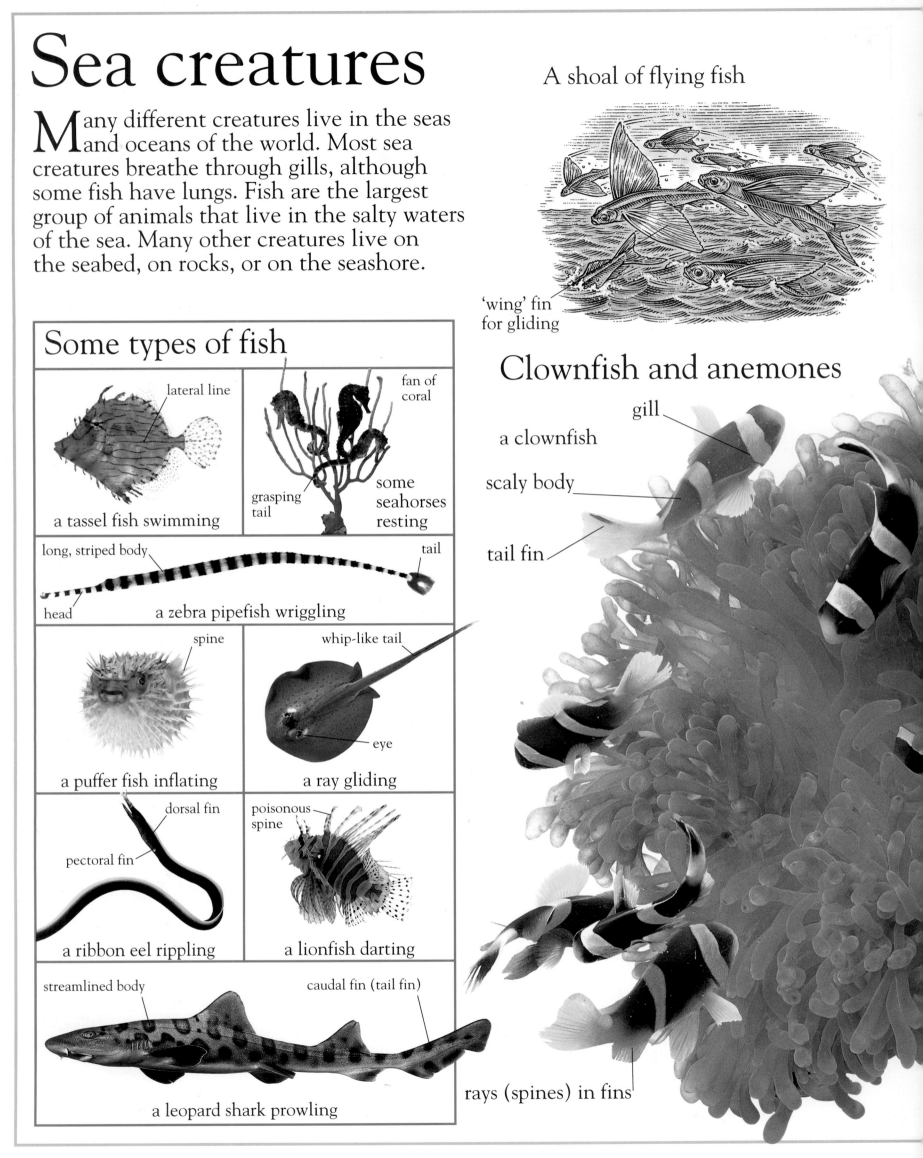

A shoal of flying fish

'wing' fin for gliding

Some types of fish

lateral line

a tassel fish swimming

fan of coral

grasping tail

some seahorses resting

long, striped body

tail

head

a zebra pipefish wriggling

spine

a puffer fish inflating

whip-like tail

eye

a ray gliding

dorsal fin

pectoral fin

a ribbon eel rippling

poisonous spine

a lionfish darting

streamlined body

caudal fin (tail fin)

a leopard shark prowling

Clownfish and anemones

a clownfish

scaly body

tail fin

gill

rays (spines) in fins

Molluscs (soft-bodied creatures)

a barnacle — a whelk shell

antenna

a hermit crab

encrusted shell

mussels on a rock

siphon (waste tube)

a big blue clam

claw

exoskeleton (outer shell)

an edible crab

a lettuce slug

mouth

frilly edge

sucker

tentacle

an octopus

dorsal (back) fin

a sea anemone

waving tentacles

barbel

transparent fin

prawn

A deep-sea angler fish

Surprising sea creatures

arm

a starfish walking

feathery tentacles

a sea cucumber crawling

soft body

trailing tentacles

a jellyfish drifting

pincer

fantail

a lobster

mouth

a sea urchin

a strawberry shrimp climbing

segmented body

Swamp and river life

Many different creatures build their homes in or near swamps and rivers. Most of these animals swim and catch their food in the water. Many plants also grow on river-banks or in muddy swamp waters.

tree trunks and branches

large, flat tail

strong teeth for gnawing

hairy body

Beavers constructing a dam on a river

A caiman in a swamp

nostril

eye with a slit

ear

scaly body

hind leg

jaws

sharp teeth

River life

river plants swaying

yellow flag iris

water arum (lily)

a brown rat diving

ear

a crayfish swimming

segmented body

tail

antenna

swimmeret (leg for swimming)

a night heron perching

beak

a pink-eared duck standing

breast

a mayfly clinging

long, jointed leg

large front wing

small back wing

tails for balance

Swamp life

piranha fish
swimming

a water hyacinth
blooming

a mud-skipper resting

leg-like
fin

gill cover

an orb weaver
spider
scuttling

orchid

a purple gallinule walking

spreading
toes

long leg

waxy,
waterproof
petal

a mangrove snake lurking

forked
tongue

two fiddler crabs fighting

giant
pincer

eye on
stalk

The life-cycle of a trout

eye

transparent
body

1 a trout egg

soft egg
shell

full yolk
sac

2 an alevin
(a baby trout)

shrinking
yolk sac

3 a very young trout

black stripes

4 a parr
(a young trout)

strong,
muscular tail

short,
wide tail

sleek,
short fur

leathery,
duck-like bill

webbed
foot

a frog

gill

speckled skin

rainbow-coloured
bar along the body

5 an adult
rainbow trout

A platypus in a river

Amphibians

All amphibians start their lives in water. Later, when they become adults, they leave the water to live on land, except for newts. All amphibians breathe through gills when they are young. However, most adult amphibians use lungs for breathing.

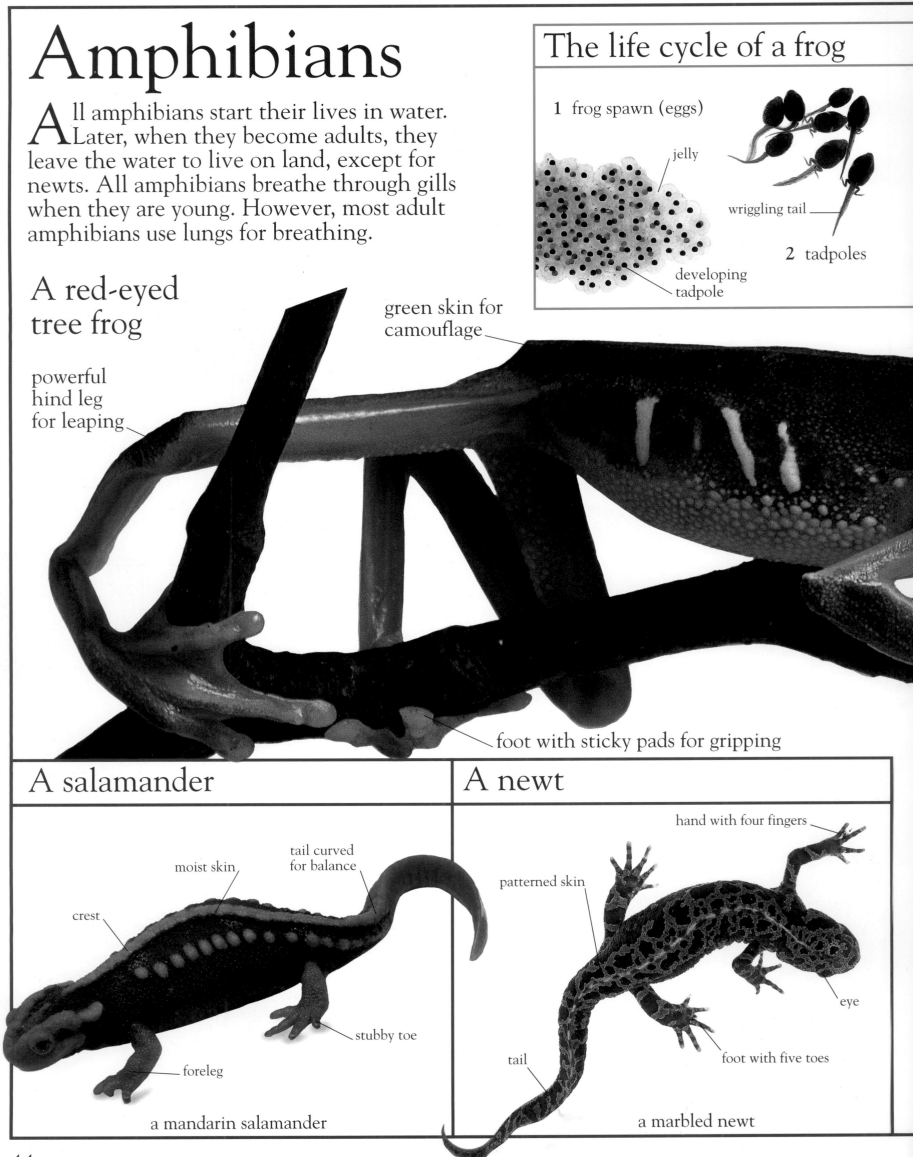

1 frog spawn (eggs)

jelly

wriggling tail

2 tadpoles

developing tadpole

A red-eyed tree frog

powerful hind leg for leaping

green skin for camouflage

foot with sticky pads for gripping

A salamander

crest

moist skin

tail curved for balance

stubby toe

foreleg

a mandarin salamander

A newt

hand with four fingers

patterned skin

eye

tail

foot with five toes

a marbled newt

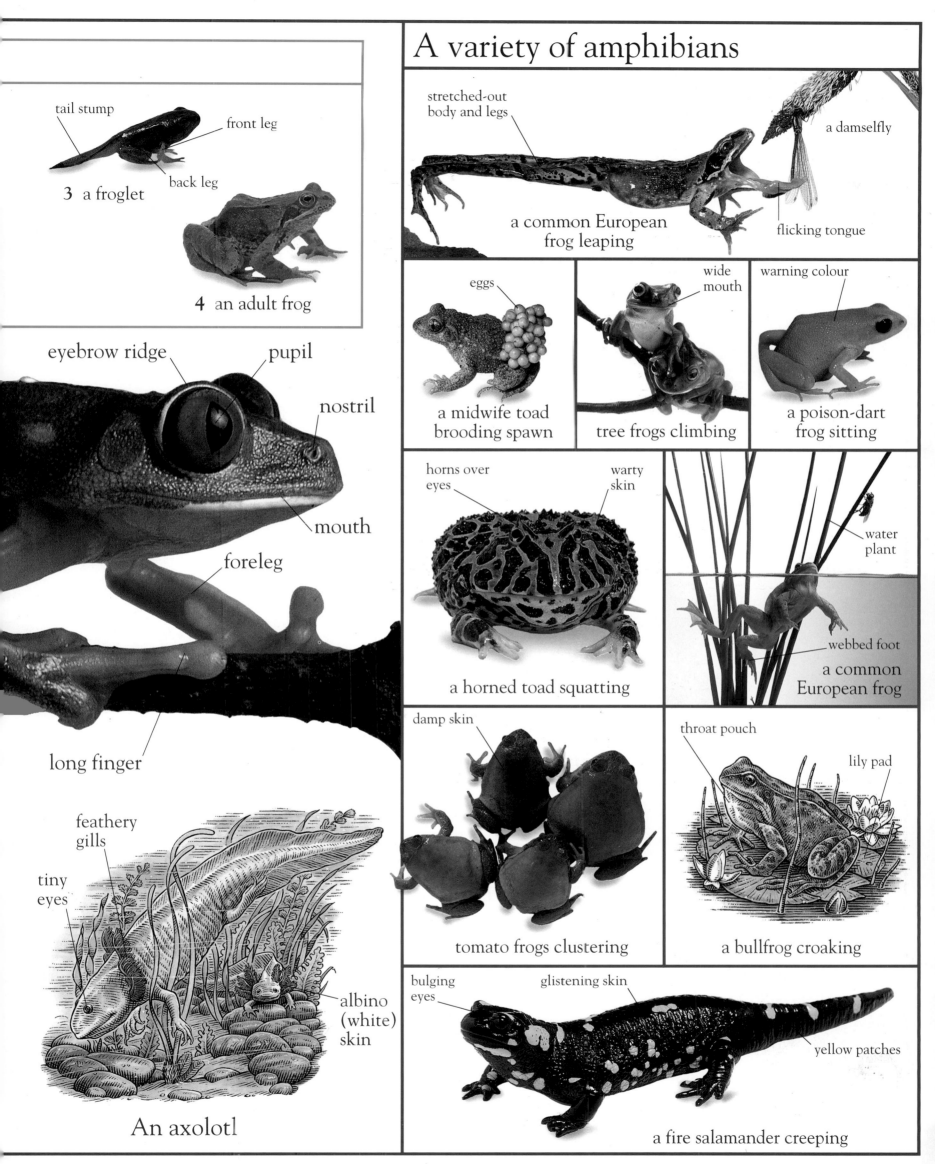

tail stump

front leg

3 a froglet

back leg

4 an adult frog

eyebrow ridge

pupil

nostril

mouth

foreleg

long finger

feathery gills

tiny eyes

albino (white) skin

An axolotl

A variety of amphibians

stretched-out body and legs

a damselfly

flicking tongue

a common European frog leaping

eggs

a midwife toad brooding spawn

wide mouth

tree frogs climbing

warning colour

a poison-dart frog sitting

horns over eyes

warty skin

a horned toad squatting

water plant

webbed foot

a common European frog

damp skin

tomato frogs clustering

throat pouch

lily pad

a bullfrog croaking

bulging eyes

glistening skin

yellow patches

a fire salamander creeping

45

Minibeasts

Most minibeasts belong to a group of animals called invertebrates. These animals do not have a backbone, but instead have a hard, outer skin, which is shed often as the animal grows. Most minibeasts hatch out of eggs. Many of them can fly, and some live in large colonies, or groups.

A swallowtail butterfly

clubbed antenna

head

thorax (upper body)

eye

abdomen (lower body)

The life cycle of a butterfly

egg

plant stalk

1 a ripe egg

mouthparts

segmented body

leg

2 a caterpillar (larva)

silk girdle

cocoon

3 a pupa or chrysalis

proboscis

damp, crumpled wing

empty cocoon

4 an adult butterfly

Different minibeasts

a scorpion scurrying

pincer

sting

furry legs

a tarantula spider crawling

a millipede wriggling

antenna

segmented body

pairs of legs

transparent wing

blood vein

a dragonfly hovering

wing case

a ladybird scuttling

wing

eye

feeler

a bluebottle fly cleaning

46

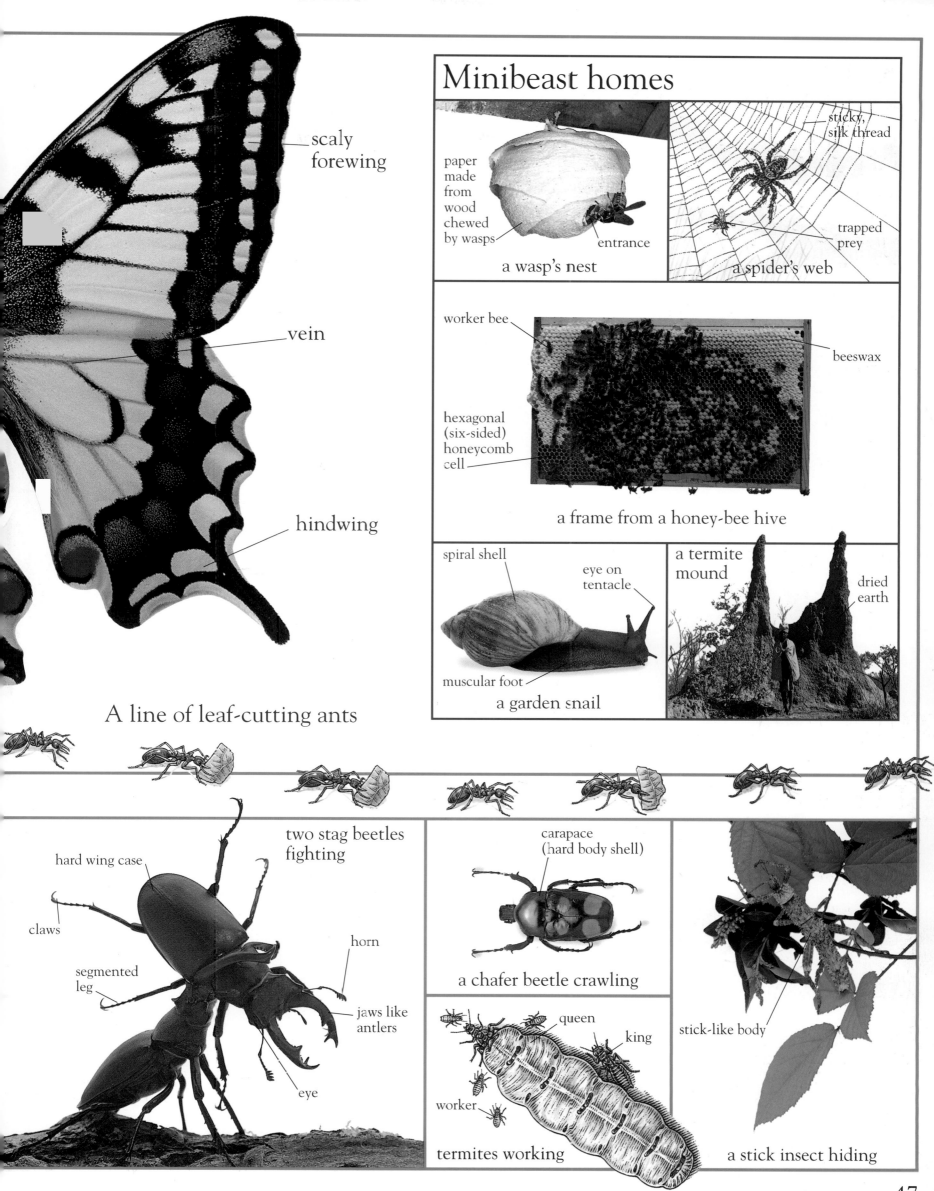

scaly
forewing

vein

hindwing

A line of leaf-cutting ants

Minibeast homes

paper
made
from
wood
chewed
by wasps

entrance

a wasp's nest

sticky,
silk thread

trapped
prey

a spider's web

worker bee

beeswax

hexagonal
(six-sided)
honeycomb
cell

a frame from a honey-bee hive

spiral shell

eye on
tentacle

muscular foot

a garden snail

a termite
mound

dried
earth

two stag beetles
fighting

hard wing case

claws

segmented
leg

horn

jaws like
antlers

eye

carapace
(hard body shell)

a chafer beetle crawling

queen

king

worker

termites working

stick-like body

a stick insect hiding

Plants

Different types of plants grow in hot, cold, wet, or dry places. Some plants are tiny, while others grow huge, such as trees. Many plants have flowers, which produce seeds to make new plants. Most plants need light, water, and air to grow well.

A hibiscus flower

stigma

stamen

pollen

petal

sepal

stalk

flower bud

veins

leaf

leaf stalk

stem

node

midrib

A variety of plants

prickly flower head

small flowers

spiky leaf

a thistle flower

spine

a Fero cactus

flower

seeds

seed head

a poppy flower

A Venus flytrap

flower head

trigger hairs

teeth

trap

trapped insect

48

frond

rhizome

root

a fern

a sunflower

ray florets

disc florets (flowers)

flower head

thick, shiny leaf

bulb

roots

a tulip bulb in bloom

tiny seed

a dandelion clock

a bee pollinating a rose

pollen sac on leg

bee sipping nectar

leaf

stem

tuber

root

a potato plant

flower

tough, waxy leaf

a waterlily

A beech tree germinating
(growing from seed)

hairy seed case

1 a beech nut

root tip

2 the seed case splits

seed husk

curled first leaves

second pair of leaves

side roots to anchor plant

first pair of leaves

main root

3 the shoot pushes upwards

4 the shoot grows into a beech tree seedling

Trees

twig

branch

needles

cone

bark

a coniferous, evergreen tree

a deciduous tree in summer

oak tree

green leaves

berry

leaf

a cluster of rowan tree berries

beech tree

bare branches

trunk

a deciduous tree in winter

49

Land environments

Different environments around the world have been created over millions of years. Some valleys were carved out by glaciers during the Ice Ages. Some mountain ranges were pushed up when sections of the Earth's surface collided. Many unique types of plants and animals have developed to live in each kind of environment.

volcanic crater peak mountain-side

In the mountains

On the plains

wildebeest
cheetah
elephant
rhinoceros
scrub tree
giraffe
zebra
kudu
the African savannah
water hole

ranch buildings
herd of cattle
gaucho (cowboy)
the South American pampas

Natural disasters

smoke
jet of lava
crater
a volcano erupting

cracked building
fissure in the ground
after an earthquake

mountaintop
snow line
slope
overhang
village

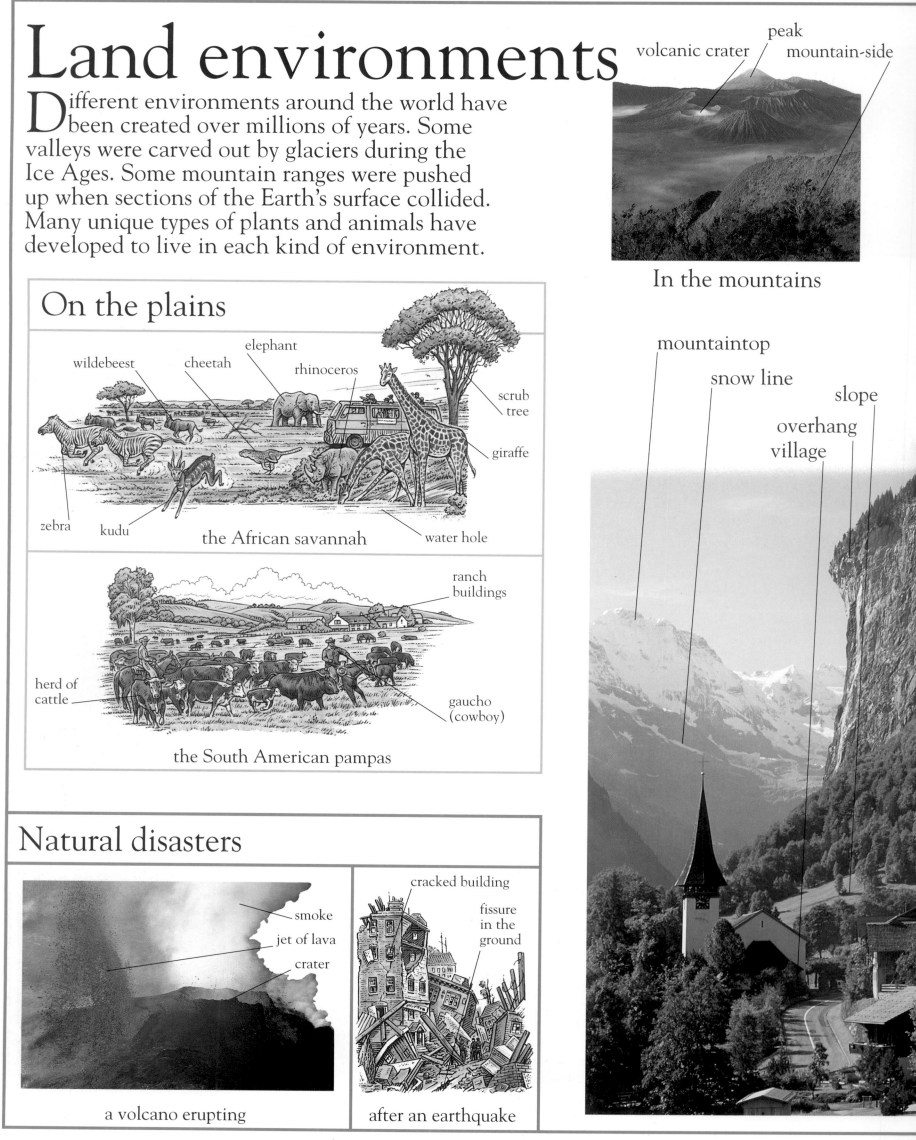

A mountain valley

waterfall

cliff

mountain ledge

forest

Forest and woodland

tall tree trunk

a redwood tree forest

a conifer tree plantation

rough scrubland

canopy

a tropical rainforest

a broadleaf wood

Desert places

sand dune

palm tree

a desert oasis

rock formation

a rocky desert

dune

camel train

a sandy desert

cactus

an arid desert

Water environments

Much of the Earth is covered by water in the form of rivers, lakes, seas, and oceans. Over many years, wind and waves wear away shorelines to form landscape features such as valleys, cliffs, and caves.

A fjord

sea inlet — steep valley side

Cold places

block of ice

an iceberg floating in the ocean

river of ice

a glacier in a mountain range

snow

a mountain avalanche

icicles on the seashore

reindeer — lichen

the frozen tundra

The coast

path · beach · rock · cave

rocky strata (layers) · surf

Water sources

boiling mud

a mud pool bubbling

steam

water jet

a geyser spurting

rocky pool

hot water springs gurgling

Rivers and lakes

a river meandering through a rainforest

rock   white water   inflatable dinghy

a river raging over rapids

reflection of mountains

a still lake

wave   rock stack   sea

cliff top

torrent

a cascading waterfall

dam

a reservoir of water

lock gates   barge

a lock on a canal

Weather

Our world, the Earth, is surrounded by a thick blanket of gases called the atmosphere. The lowest layer of the atmosphere is constantly swirling, and this creates the different forms of our weather – from warm, sunny days to raging thunderstorms and hurricanes.

Some types of weather

fog

a dull, foggy day

lightning

a wild thunderstorm

a freezing cold day

a blustery, windy day

mist

a damp, rainy day

blue sky

a hot, sunny day

Landscape after a thunderstorm

bright sunlight

horizon

Forecasting the weather

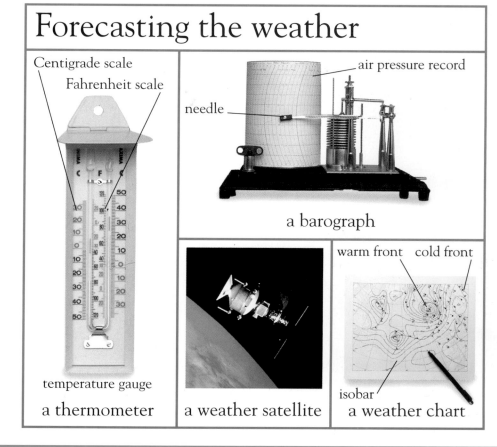

Centigrade scale
Fahrenheit scale

temperature gauge

a thermometer

air pressure record

needle

a barograph

a weather satellite

warm front   cold front

isobar
a weather chart

rainbow

storm clouds

blue sky

Different types of clouds

altocumulus clouds

cirrus clouds

lenticular clouds

cumulus clouds

A weather station

hygrometer (air humidity measure)

anemometer (wind measure)

meteorologist (weather scientist)

Extremes of weather

a torrential flood

cracked earth

a searing drought

wind funnel

cloud base

a swirling tornado

tidal wave

a violent hurricane

snow drift

after a blizzard

a raging dust storm

Early life on Earth

The first plants and animals lived on the Earth over 700 million years ago. Since then, many species have developed and died out again, such as the dinosaurs. Dinosaurs lived on the Earth for about 165 million years, but became extinct (died out) long before the first humans appeared.

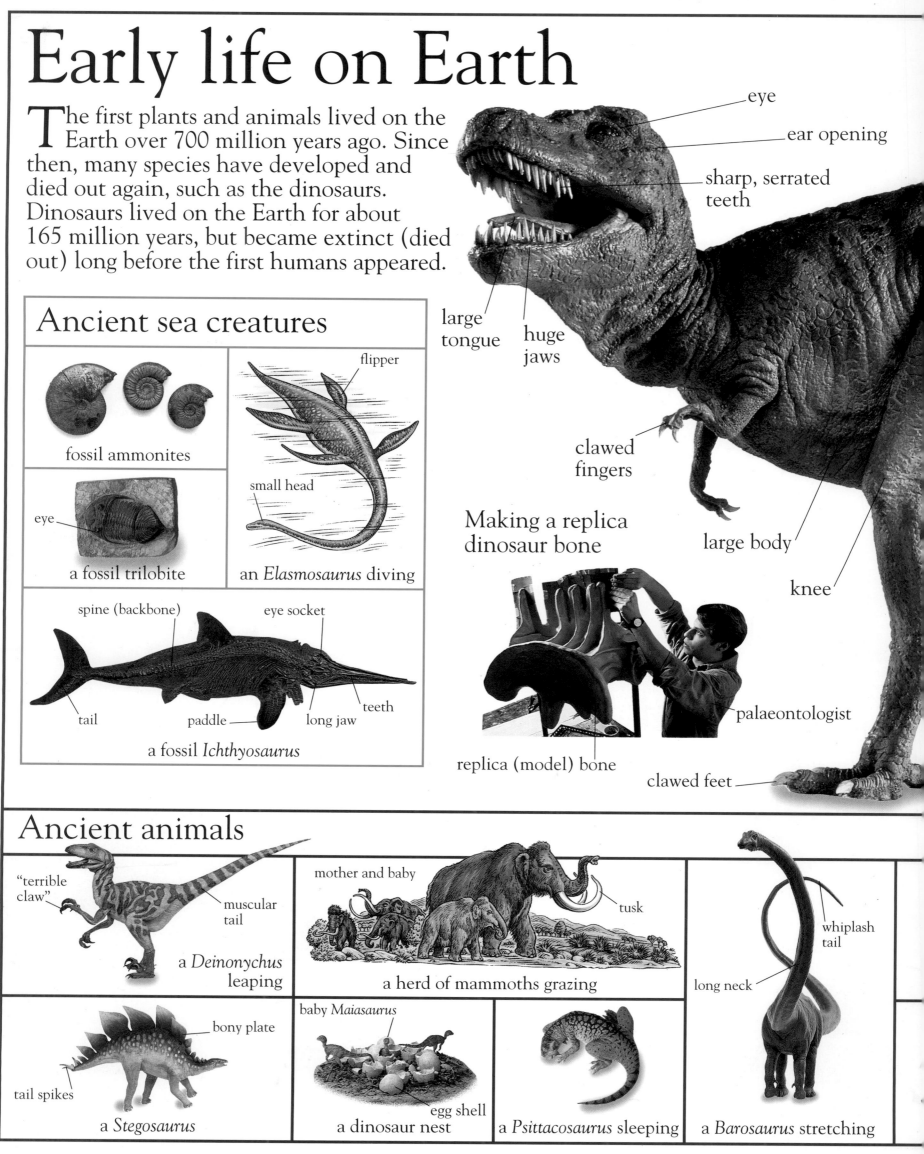

eye

ear opening

sharp, serrated teeth

large tongue

huge jaws

clawed fingers

large body

knee

Ancient sea creatures

fossil ammonites

flipper

small head

eye

a fossil trilobite

an *Elasmosaurus* diving

spine (backbone)

eye socket

tail

paddle

long jaw

teeth

a fossil *Ichthyosaurus*

Making a replica dinosaur bone

palaeontologist

replica (model) bone

clawed feet

Ancient animals

"terrible claw"

muscular tail

a *Deinonychus* leaping

tail spikes

bony plate

a *Stegosaurus*

mother and baby

tusk

a herd of mammoths grazing

baby *Maiasaurus*

egg shell

a dinosaur nest

a *Psittacosaurus* sleeping

whiplash tail

long neck

a *Barosaurus* stretching

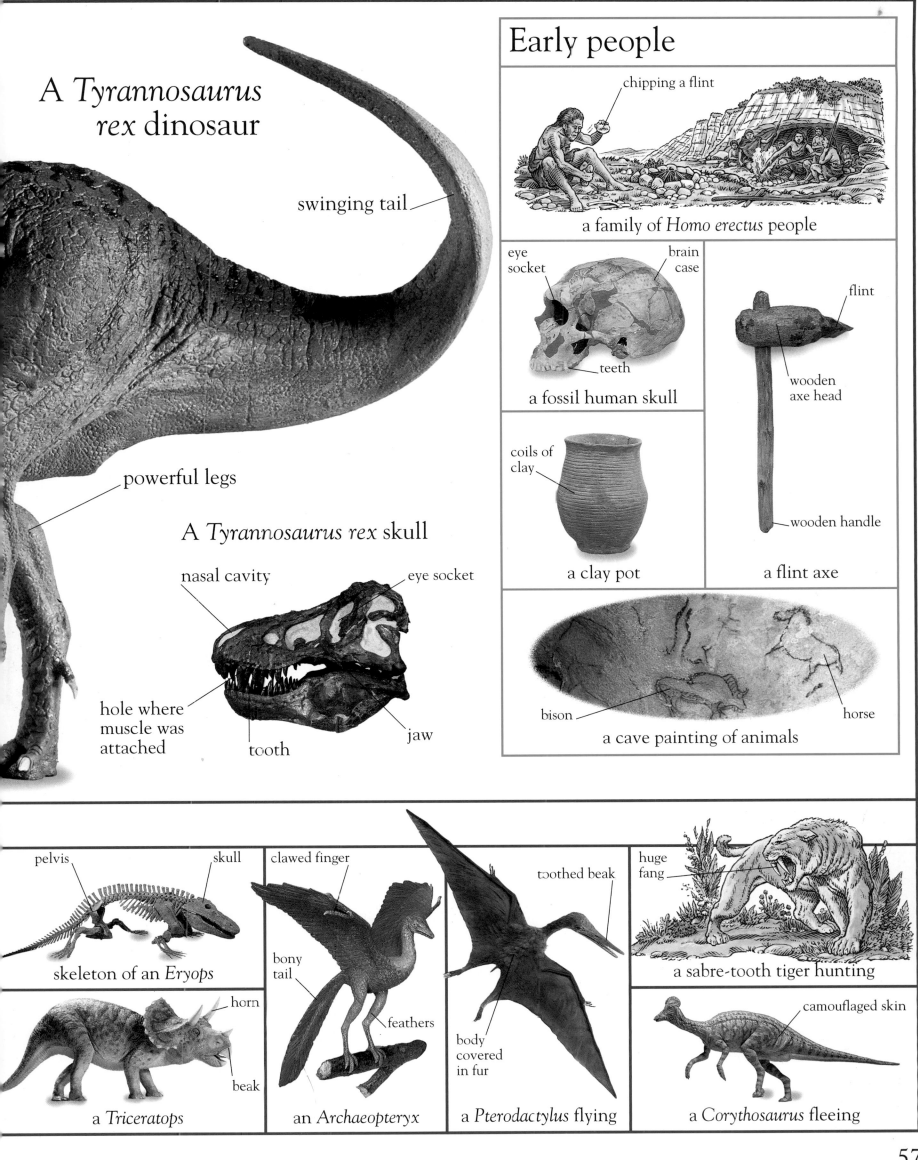

A *Tyrannosaurus rex* dinosaur

swinging tail

powerful legs

A *Tyrannosaurus rex* skull

nasal cavity

eye socket

hole where muscle was attached

tooth

jaw

Early people

chipping a flint

a family of *Homo erectus* people

eye socket

brain case

teeth

a fossil human skull

flint

wooden axe head

wooden handle

a flint axe

coils of clay

a clay pot

bison

horse

a cave painting of animals

pelvis

skull

skeleton of an *Eryops*

horn

beak

a *Triceratops*

clawed finger

bony tail

feathers

an *Archaeopteryx*

toothed beak

body covered in fur

a *Pterodactylus* flying

huge fang

a sabre-tooth tiger hunting

camouflaged skin

a *Corythosaurus* fleeing

Space

The first artificial satellite was launched into orbit around our planet, the Earth, in 1957. Today, different types of spacecraft regularly blast off from the Earth. They place satellites into orbit and carry astronauts or equipment such as space probes out into space.

An astronaut

pressure helmet

sun visor

camera

thruster control

thruster

Out in space

a galaxy of stars

an eclipse of the Sun
Sun (behind)
Moon (in front)

a comet

a black hole

a nebula (mist of stars)

a constellation of stars

Planets in our solar system

Pluto
Neptune
Uranus
Saturn
Jupiter
Mars
Venus
Earth
Mercury
Sun (a star)

Walking on the Moon

Earth

radio aerial

lunar (Moon) buggy

rake for collecting rock samples

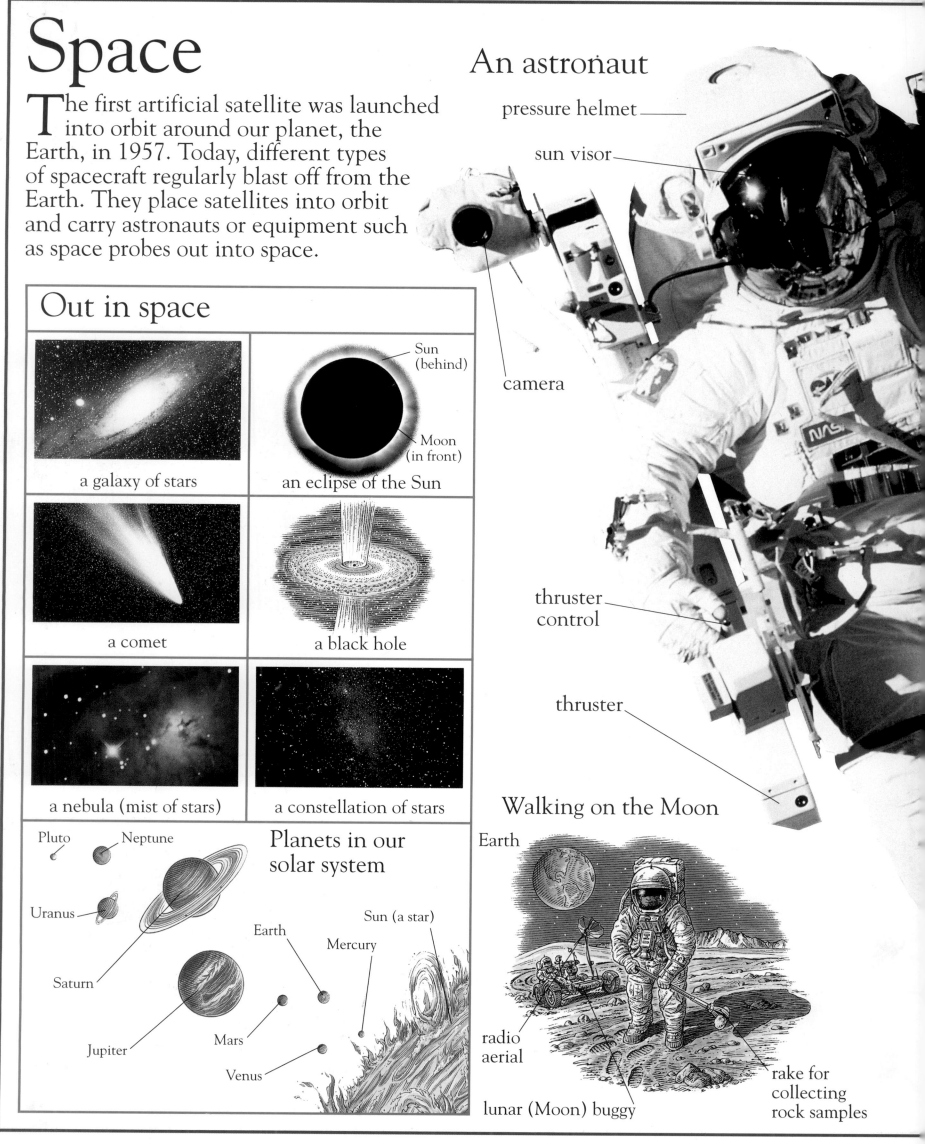

Manned Manoeuvring
Unit (MMU)

safety harness

space glove

hand control

padded oversuit

Space machines

escape tower

command
module

lunar
module

engine

fuel
tank

engine   fin

a space rocket

solar
panel

a space telescope

splashdown

a command module

antenna   sensors

gas nozzle

an unmanned spacecraft

a space shuttle blasting off

Life on board a space ship

sleeping-bag

body
strap

space bed

sleeping

instrument
deck

treadmill   air lock

exercising

Index

T his index shows on which page you can find each word and its picture in this dictionary. You can also use the index to find words and to check spellings when you are writing.

ACKNOWLEDGEMENTS

Dorling Kindersley would like to thank the following for their help:

Picture credits

t=top b=bottom m=middle l=left r=right c=centre b=below a=above (b=bottom only if it comes first in the sequence)

Air 2 Air front cover tr, spine, 33tl; J.Allan Cash 10bl, br, 11bl, 20cl, cb, 21tl, crb, 22br, bl, 23ca, br, bl, 58clb; Bruce Coleman Ltd/Gerald Cubitt 50tr; Robert Harding Picture Library 11br, 21tr, cl, br, 22–23c, 22bc, 29cla, 52bl, 53bra, 54c, 55tl; Holt Studios/Nigel Catlin 24cla, 25tr, /Mary Cherry 24c; The Hutchison Library 21c, /Bernard Regent 23cra, /M.Von Puttkamer 54cl, bl; The Image Bank/Jurgen Vogt 8bl, 10–11c, /Paul J. Sutton 19bc, 21cb, 33crb, /Trevor Wood 51tc, Frank Whitney 54cb, Cliff Feulner 55bcl, /Ira Block 55bcr; London Underground Ltd 29tl; NASA 58–59c, 58bl, 59cr; NHPA 47cr; PGL Adventures 19br; Science Photo Library/NASA 58tl, cl, cla; Tony Stone Images 6bl, br, 22cb, clb, 50bl, 50–51c, 51cra, crb, 51bc, 52tl, cl, br, 53cl, 54tl, bcl, 54–55c, 55cl, tc, tr, ca; Jean Vertut 57cr; World Pictures 51br, 52/53c, 53tl, cr, bc; ZEFA 19bl, 20–21c, 21cr, 23c, 25tl, 29br, 51tr, 55br.

Additional photography
Peter Anderson, Geoff Brightling, Jane Burton, Peter Chadwick, Simon Clay, Andy Crawford, Philip Dowell, John Downes, Mike Dunning, Andreas Von Einsiedel, Neil Fletcher, Lynton Gardiner, Philip Gatward, Frank Greenaway, Finbar Hawkins, John Heseltine, John Holmes, Colin Keates, Dave King, Bob Langrish, Cyril Laubscher, Richard Leeney, John Lepine, Mike Linley, Andrew McRobb, Ray Moller, David Murray, National Maritime Museum, Ian O'Leary, Stephen Oliver, Oxford Scientific Films, Daniel Pangbourne, Roger Phillips, Susanna Price, Barlow Reid, Tim Ridley, David Rudkin, Science Museum, Jules Selmes, Karl Shone, Steve Shott, James Stephenson, Clive Streeter, Kim Taylor, Matthew Ward, Paul Williams, Alex Wilson, Jerry Young.

Models
Sarah Ashun, Jodie Attreed, Jade Bailey, Monica Byles, Hannah Capelton, Jayda Ceylan, Reshmee Doolub, Gemmel Haines, James Henderson, Oliver Jenkins, Christina and Luke Kyprianou, Jasmine McAtee, Kim Ng, Peter Radcliffe, Maxwell Ralph, Tebedge Ricketts, John Walden, Martin Wilson.

Additional acknowledgements
Valya Alexander; BBC TV Film Services, Wood Lane, London; Dixon's electrical store; Graphical Innovations for typesetting; Hamleys toyshop, 188–196 Regent Street, London W1R 6BT (0171 – 734 3161); picnic hamper on page 13 from John Lewis, Oxford Street, London (0171 – 629 7711); Lunn Poly Travel Agency; National Meteorological Library, Bracknell, Berks.; Mark Richards; Chris Scollen; Lee Simmons; Martin Wilson.